W9-DHK-239

The Abolition of Slavery

Fighting for a Free America

Titles in *The American Saga* series

The Abolition of Slavery
Fighting for a Free America
0-7660-2605-1

America as a World Power
From the Spanish-American War to Today
0-7660-2606-X

Colonial America
Building Toward Independence
0-7660-2569-1

The History of U.S. Immigration
Coming to America
0-7660-2574-8

The Industrial Revolution
Manufacturing a Better America
0-7660-2571-3

The New Deal
Pulling America Out of the Great Depression
0-7660-2570-5

The Struggle for Equality
Women and Minorities in America
0-7660-2573-X

The Transcontinental Railroad and Westward Expansion
Chasing the American Frontier
0-7660-2572-1

The Abolition of Slavery

Fighting for a Free America

Suzanne Cloud Tapper

Enslow Publishers, Inc.
40 Industrial Road
Box 398
Berkeley Heights, NJ 07922
USA

http://www.enslow.com

Library of Congress Cataloging-in-Publication Data:

Cloud Tapper, Suzanne.
    The abolition of slavery : fighting for a free America / Suzanne
Cloud Tapper.
        p. cm. — (The American saga)
    Includes bibliographical references and index.
    ISBN-10: 0-7660-2605-1
        1. Antislavery movements—United States—History—19th century—
Juvenile literature. 2. Abolitionists—United States—History—19th
century—Juvenile literature. I. Title. II. Series.
    E449.C636 2006
    973.7'11—dc22

                                    2006001739

ISBN-13: 978-0-7660-2605-6

Printed in the United States of America

10 9 8 7 6 5 4 3 2

To Our Readers:
We have done our best to make sure all Internet Addresses in this book were
active and appropriate when we went to press. However, the author and the
publisher have no control over and assume no liability for the material available
on those Internet sites or on other Web sites they may link to. Any comments or
suggestions can be sent by e-mail to comments@enslow.com or to the address on
the back cover.

Illustration Credits: Abraham Lincoln Presidential Library, p. 14; akg
images, pp. 3 (middle), 99; Board of Directors at the Levi Coffin House,
p. 74; The Bridgeman Art Library, pp. 24, 73; Enslow Publishers, Inc., p. 72;
Getty Images, p. 80; The Library of Congress, pp. 3 (left and right), 8, 17,
27, 34, 40, 44, 47, 51, 56, 68, 77, 86, 88, 92, 94, 96; ©Mary Evans Picture
Library/The Image Works, pp. 66, 89; North Wind Picture Archives, pp. 11,
15, 59, 81; Paul Collins, p. 78; ©Roger-Viollet/Topham/The Image Works,
p. 22; ©Topham/The Image Works, p. 19.

Cover Illustration: akg-images.

Contents

The Death of Elijah Lovejoy

The lynch mob's ringleaders piled firewood around the feet of a free African American from Pittsburgh, Pennsylvania, named Francis McIntosh. The frightened boatman had been dragged from a jail cell and chained to a locust tree. Even though historians are unsure what happened next, local legend has it that the mayor's daughter cheerfully lit the fire around McIntosh's feet that spring in 1836, in St. Louis, Missouri. No matter who lit the fire, thousands watched as McIntosh was slowly burned to death. This grim exhibition was not covered by the usual southern press, but by a reporter sent from the *St. Louis Observer*, a new religious weekly newspaper whose editor was Elijah Lovejoy:

> He said not a word till he felt that the flames had seized him. He then uttered an awful howl, attempting to sing and pray, then hung his head and suffered in silence . . . his eyes burned out of his head . . . someone in the crowd proposed to end his misery by shooting him. But it was replied that he was already out of his pain. "No, No, cried

The Abolition of Slavery

"LAWLESS" BURNING OF MEN "BY THE MANY."

April 28, 1836, in St. Louis, Mo., a black man named McIntosh, who had stabbed an officer, that had arrested him, was seized by the multitude, and fastened to a tree *in the midst of the city,* in the open day, and in the presence of an immense throng of citizens, was burnt to death. The Alton (Ill.) Telegraph, in its account of the scene says :

"All was silent while they were piling wood around their victim ; when the flames seized upon him he uttered an awful howl, attempted to sing and pray, and then hung his head and suffered in silence, except in the following instance :—After the flames had surrounded their prey, his eyes burnt out of his head, and his mouth seemingly parched to a cinder, some one in the crowd, proposed to put an end to his misery by shooting him, when it was replied, 'that would be of no use, since he was already out of pain.' 'No, no,' said the wretch, I am suffering as much as ever ; shoot me, shoot me.' 'No, no,' said one, 'he shall not be shot. *I would sooner slacken the fire, if that would increase his misery ;*' and the man who said this was, as we understand, an OFFICER OF JUSTICE."

The St. Louis correspondent of a New York paper adds :—"The shrieks and groans of the victim were loud and piercing, and to observe one limb after another drop into the fire was awful indeed. I visited the place this morning ; only a part of his head and body were left."

Hon. Luke E. Lawless, Judge, of the Circuit Court of Missouri, at its session, in St. Louis, some months after, decided that since the burning of McIntosh was the act, directly or by countenance, of a *majority* of citizens, it is a 'case which transcends the jurisdiction,' of the Grand Jury !

The 'New Orleans Post,' of June 7, 1836, publishes the following :—

"We understand, that a negro man was lately condemned, by the mob, to be BURNED OVER A SLOW FIRE, which was put into execution at Grand Gulf, Mississippi, for murdering a black woman and her master."

"Tuscaloosa, Ala., June 20, 1827.—Last week a Mr. M'Neilly charged a slave with theft. M'Neilly, and his brother, seized him, and were about to chastise him, when the negro stabbed M'Neilly. The negro was taken before a justice, who *waived his authority.* A crowd collected, *and he acted as president of the mob,* and put the vote, when it was decided he should be immediately *burnt to death.*" He was led to the tree, a large quantity of pine knots placed around him, the fatal torch applied to the pile, and the miserable being was in a short time burned to ashes. This is the SECOND negro who has been THUS put to death, without judge or Jury, in this county."—African Observer, for August, 1827.

This article about the burning of Francis McIntosh appeared in the *Anti-Slavery Almanac* in 1840.

[McIntosh] . . . I am not. I am suffering as much as ever. Shoot me! Shoot me!" . . . One of the fiends standing by the roasting sacrifice [said], "No, he shall not be shot. I would sooner slack the fire if that would increase his misery."

No one dared, for whatever reason, to stop the agony as the flames burned the man for twenty minutes more. A New York newspaper reporter wrote that the piercing cries of McIntosh were "awful indeed . . . as one limb after another drop[ped] into the fire . . ."[1]

When the murderers of Francis McIntosh were brought to court, the local judge, Luke Lawless, ruled that no crime had been committed. The rule of the mob represented the will of the people, so the killers went free. Editor Elijah Lovejoy poked savage fun at the judge's name and condemned Lawless' verdict in print. Because Lovejoy decided to speak out against the mob by writing about the lynching of Francis McIntosh, he was driven out of the city of St. Louis.

Early Years

Elijah Lovejoy was one of eight children and the son of a minister from Kennebec County, Maine. Born in 1802, Lovejoy was intelligent and likeable. His father thought Elijah might just be a minister, too. However, after Lovejoy graduated from college in 1826, he set off westward like so many other young men at the time. He settled in St. Louis, a bustling crossroads where everyone seemed to come together before making their way west. Lovejoy needed a job immediately, and St. Louis needed reporters. Within a short time, Elijah Lovejoy was not only working at the *St. Louis Times*; he became the editor.

In the 1800s, the position of editor involved almost every task needed to run a newspaper: taking out the trash, setting printing type, selling advertising, and sending reporters to cover interesting stories.

After five years, Lovejoy decided to go back to school. In 1832, he returned east to Princeton University in New Jersey and spent a year studying religion. But Lovejoy still felt the pull of the newspaper business. Friends back in St. Louis convinced him that the rough and tumble world of St. Louis "riverboatmen, traders, and drifters" needed a religious weekly newspaper.[2] His friends raised twelve hundred dollars to buy him a printing press and guaranteed him a salary of five hundred dollars a year. So, in November 1833, the *St. Louis Observer* was born.

Trouble in St. Louis

Elijah Lovejoy loved reading the newspaper *The Liberator*. William Lloyd Garrison, an abolitionist, was the newspaper's editor. Lovejoy agreed with *The Liberator*'s ideas. It so affected Lovejoy that, even though Missouri was a slave state, he began publishing editorials in the *Observer* that questioned the institution of slavery. The articles Lovejoy wrote were mildly critical at first and none of the readers said anything. But the more Lovejoy thought about slavery, the angrier he became. The stories in his paper became stronger and made the people in St. Louis feel more uncomfortable.[3]

Soon, the publishers of the *St. Louis Observer* called a meeting to remind Lovejoy that they wanted their paper to be a strictly religious paper. Slavery stories were not to be covered. The people reading the paper were becoming very irritated that their religious sincerity was being challenged. According to the local community, slavery was not about morality. To them, slavery was an economic issue. They wanted Lovejoy to stop writing about it. But Lovejoy said

In the 1830s, Elijah Lovejoy denounced slave owners in front of Congress.

that the Constitution of the United States and the constitution of Missouri gave him a right to free speech. He wrote, ". . . and whether I exercise that right or not is for me, not for the mob, to decide."[4]

Shortly thereafter, Francis McIntosh was lynched. Elijah Lovejoy broke a traditional rule of southern journalism—he reported on the murders of black citizens by whites and described every gory detail. Then, in July, when the mob leaders were being tried in court, Lovejoy made fun of the judge and the entire court proceeding. This made some of his readers even more outraged. The people in the town threatened Lovejoy, and he realized he had to leave.

In his last issue of the *St. Louis Observer,* he announced he was moving the paper to Alton, Illinois, which was right across the Mississippi River. Lovejoy had the support of antislavery people there who would help him transfer the paper to its new home. Lastly, he wrote that another reason he was leaving was because he feared his wife and his children would be hurt by the mob. He could not take a chance with their safety. The very night of Lovejoy's announcement of the move, a mob broke into the *Observer*'s offices and smashed everything—including the printing press. Lovejoy left St. Louis in July 1836, he ordered a new press to be delivered to his new address.[5]

Making a Stand in Alton

Trouble started the minute Lovejoy arrived in Alton. His increasing passion about slavery began to stir up a lot of local opposition. By spring 1837, the *Alton Observer* was clearly being seen by the community as an abolitionist paper. Soon, Alton citizens organized a mass meeting and warned him not to print stories about slavery. Lovejoy stated again that no public meeting "could dictate what sentiments should not be discussed in a duly authorized newspaper."[6] Lovejoy was threatened twice in August 1837. Then, like in St. Louis, his offices were broken into and his press destroyed. He asked the general public in Illinois to help. Many people there supported free speech, so they quickly donated funds for a new press. However, it was destroyed on arrival that September. Lovejoy pleaded for more money to buy a fourth printing press. The threats continued.

The mob attacked the warehouse, throwing stones and breaking windows.

The *Alton Observer*'s fourth press arrived in November 1837. It was put in a warehouse for safekeeping until it could be moved to the newspaper offices. Lovejoy was aware that some people were planning to destroy it again. A few of his friends armed themselves and stayed in the warehouse to protect the printing press.

ALTON OBSERVER.
Extra.

ALTON, SEPTEMBER 28, 1837.

STATE CONVENTION.

The present aspect of the slavery question in this country, and especially in this State, is of commanding interest to us all. No question is, at the present time, exerting so strong an influence upon the public mind as this. The whole land is agitated by it. We cannot, nor would we remain indifferent spectators in the midst of developements so vitally interesting to us all, as those which are daily taking place in relation to the system of American Slavery.— We have duties to perform, as Christians and as Patriots, which call for united wisdom, counsel and energy of action.

The undersigned would, therefore, respectfully call a meeting of the friends of the slave and of free discussion in the State of Illinois, to meet in Convention at UPPER ALTON, ON THE LAST THURSDAY OF OCTOBER. It is intended that this Convention should consist of all those in the State who believe that the system of American Slavery is sinful and ought to be immediately abandoned, however diversified may be their views in other respects. It is desirable that the opponents in this State of Domestic Slavery—all who ardently long and pray to witness its *immediate* abolition, should co-operate together in their efforts to accomplish it. We therefore hope that all such will make it a point of duty to attend the Convention, not thereby feeling that they are pledged to any particular course of action, but that they may receive as well as impart the benefit of mutual counsel and advice.

It is earnestly to be hoped that there will be a full attendance at the Convention. Let all who feel deeply interested in this cause, not only attend themselves, but stir up their neighbors to attend also. And let each one remember that this call cannot be repeated. But for the destruction of the "OBSERVER" press it would have been circulated some time since. It is hoped, that it will have time to circulate in season to bring together a large number of our friends from all parts of the State.

QUINCY.

John Burns
Richard Eells
Levi Stillman
Rufus Brown
Ezra Fisher,
Peter R. Borien,
Charles Burnham
Evan Williams
John R. George,
Henry Thompson
Myron Gaylord,
Jery Platt
Edward Platt
Lucius Kingman
Charles Howland
J. B. Brown
J. T. Holmes,
J. R. Beston
Edward L. Turner
Ross Hood
Joseph Craig, jr.
Andrew Segur
Alvin T. Smith
David Nelson
Levi B. Allen
John Benson
George Westgate
Benjamin Bran
Samuel Winter
Amos Bancroft
Erastus Benton
Edward Turner
Frederick Carrott
Loren Harkness
H. H. Snow
Willard Keyes
H. L. Montandon
Henry Barrett
James Stobie
Henry Maire
George Ogden
Charles Horhman
Francis Pearson
Henry C. Pitkin
E. B. Kimball
Henry H. Hoffman
James M. Flack
Strong Burnell
R. P. Vance
Lewis Faxon
Peter Felt

John E Morey
Peter M'Worthy
Bernard McKenzie
Porter Smith
A. C. Root
Artemas Ward
Charles Brown
Julius Brown
Elijah Ballard
Ebenezer White

Fairfield, Adams co.
J. B. Chittenden
W. H. Hubbard
William Kirby,
D. Bartholomew
Rufus Hubbard
Caleb Smith
Benjamin Baldwin
J. W. Cook
C. Talcott
Anson M. Hubbard

Chatham, Sangamon county.
L. N. Ransom
Josiah Porter
H. T. White
Cornelius Lyman
A. Stockwell

Peoria.
Jeremiah Porter,
Aaron Russell
Joseph Gambell
Alfred Castler
A. S. Castler
Samuel Castler
Wm. E. Castler
Wm. Guilford jr.
Calvin Winslow
James Clark
Joseph Thompson
Abraham Vauops
John M. Smith
H. W. Reynolds
J. R. Stanton
Nathaniel Warden
John Reynolds
Henry Little
Moses Pettingill

Galesburgh.
Nehemiah H. Long
Thomas Simmons
Luther Gay
Erastus Swift
H. H. May
Hugh Conger
John Kendall
Adoniram Kendall
Patrick Dunn
John McMullin
Wm. Holyoke
Levi Sanderson
Eli Farnham
Leonard Chappell
C. W. Gilbert
W. P. Hamlin
Nehemiah West
Abraham Tyler
Geo. Avery
John West
Samuel Tompkins
Sylvanus Ferris
James Bunce
Elisha H King
Abel Goodell
Warren Goodell

Henry Ferris
Wm S Gale
James Waters
Samuel Hitchcock
Lucien Mills
George Ferris
Lorenius Conger
Henry Wilcox
Ephraim P Nail
Enos Pomeroy
John Waters
Geo. W. Gale,
Brainard Orton
Miles Smith

Hennepin.
W. M. Stuart
S. D. Laughlin
J. N. Laughlin
James G. Dunlavy
Stephen D. Willis

Springfield.
Erastus Wright
Z. Hallock
E. B. Hawley
R. P. Abel
Roswell Abel
W. M. Cowgill
Isaac Bancroft jr
J. C. Bancroft
Oliver B. Culver
J. B. Watson
J. Stephenson
C. B. Francis
J. G. Rawson
Joseph Taney
Edmund R. Wiley
James Pratt
Josiah Francis
Elisha Taber
Geo. N. Kendall
S. Conant
E. W. Thayer

Farmington, Sangamon county.
Peter Bates
Asahel Stone
Azel Lyman
Alvan Lyman
Harooldus Estabrook
Ezra Lyman
Bishop Seely
B. B. More
Jay Slater
H. P. Lyman
Oliver Bates
Stephen Child
O. L. Stone
A. S. Lyman
Joel Buckman
John Lyman
T. Galt

Waverly, Morgan co.
Dr. Isaac H. Brown

Carlinville, Ill.
J. W. Buchanan

Alton.
C. W. Hunter
Royal Weller
P. B. Whipple
W. H. Chappell
Elijah P. Lovejoy
Owen Lovejoy
George Kimball
E. Beall

Moses Forbes
S. E. Moore
E. Upham
James Mansfield
J. S. Clark
G. Holton
Rev. H. Loomis
J. Carpenter
E. Dennison
John Bates
H. Sterns
J. Thompson
Thomas Lippincott,
T. B. Hurlburt
F. W. Graves

Pleasant Grove, Taze-well co.
Julius Bascom

Washington, Taze-well co.
James P. Scott
F. R Whipple
Romulus Barnes

Pekin, Tazewell co.
Nathaniel Bailey
Joseph Booden
David Bailey

Monmouth, Warren co
George H. Wright

Jacksonville.
Wm. Carter
E. Wolcott
Timothy Chamberlain
Thos W. Melendy
Jeremiah Graves
Maro M. L. Reed
C. B. Barton
J. G. Edwards
Martin Hart
C. B. Blood
R. W. Patterson
D. D. Nelson
W. Jones
M Hicks
W. T. Mills
A. B. Hitchcock
S. Wells
J. S. Graves
R. S. Kendall
E. Scofield

Sand Prairie, Taze-well co.
Lyman Harkness
R. M. Pearson
George Pyle
Lemuel Holton
Samuel C. Woodrow
Thomas Lawrie
Wm. Woodrow
A. W. Estabrook
H. D. Chipman
Ralph Perry
R. Grosvenor
L. Dunham
Thos. C. Kenworthy
Wm. S. Burnett
S. Chandler
Ebenezer Carter
E Beecher

I hope that in view of the fact, that the "Observer" Press has been THREE TIMES destroyed in Alton, in the space of little more than one year, it will not be deemed out of place, for me, in this special manner to call upon the friends of law, of order, of equal rights, and of free discussion, to rally at the proposed Convention in numbers and with a zeal corresponding to the urgency of the crisis. Our dearest rights are at stake—rights, which as American Citizens ought to be dearer to us than our lives. Take away the right of FREE DISCUSSION—the right under the laws, freely to utter and publish such sentiments as duty to God and the fulfilment of a good conscience may require, and we have nothing left to struggle for. Come up then, ye friends of God and man! come up to the rescue, and let it be known whether the spirit of freedom yet presides over the destinies of Illinois, or whether the "dark spirit" of Slavery has already so far diffused itself through our community, as that the discussion of the inalienable rights of man can no longer be tolerated.

ELIJAH P. LOVEJOY.

Alton. September 27, 1837.

On September 28, 1837, the *Alton Observer* announced a meeting of an Illinois abolitionist group.

Rioters set the warehouse where Lovejoy's press was stored on fire.

At nine o'clock at night on November 7, a mob formed. They were going to march on the warehouse. The mayor and the state attorney general tried to break up the mob, but could not. The mob attacked the warehouse, throwing stones and breaking windows. Eventually it was set afire. Lovejoy's friends tried to put out the flames. Then, a barrage of bullets hit Lovejoy as he stood in an open doorway. He fell down dead. Even though both sides had guns, it is not known whether Lovejoy was armed when he was shot. The mob finished burning the building, pummeled the printing press to pieces, and threw it in the river.[7]

A Country Divided

The news of Lovejoy's murder rumbled throughout the country. Some proslavery people said that Elijah Lovejoy deserved what happened to him. Some compared the mob that killed Lovejoy to the patriots that dumped tea into Boston Harbor during the Boston Tea Party.

In Boston, Massachusetts, on December 8, 1837, abolitionists packed into Faneuil Hall to hear speakers denounce Lovejoy's death. Then, a voice was heard from the gallery. Everyone looked up and recognized James Austin, the attorney general of Massachusetts. He asked to speak. The request was granted, and, to the horror of many in the room, Austin argued against Elijah Lovejoy. He said the mob in Alton had been right in what they did; Lovejoy had threatened the safety of his community. Austin compared Lovejoy's editorials against slavery to someone advocating that wild beasts be turned loose in Boston. Most of the crowd in the hall were angry—one man especially so.[8]

A young man, only twenty-six years old, stepped up in front of a crowd for the first time in his life to defend the brave editor. He was a compelling speaker. Against the ravings of James Austin, this sandy-haired lawyer was quiet, but forceful. His name was Wendell Phillips. Part of what he had to say was:

> The difference between the excitements of those days [of the American Revolution] and our own . . . is simply this: the men of that day went for the right, as secured by the laws. They were the people rising to sustain the laws and Constitution . . . the rioters of our day go for their own wills, right or wrong . . . Elijah Lovejoy was not only defending the freedom of the press, but he was under his own roof,

in arms with the sanction of civil authority . . . When he fell, civil authority was trampled underfoot.[9]

On that night, the abolitionist career of Wendell Phillips was born and he soon became a leader of the New England antislavery movement. He would devote his entire life to unpopular social causes including women's right to vote and the ending of the death penalty.

The abolitionist movement did not start with the death of Elijah Lovejoy. He was just considered to be the first white martyr of the movement. Abolitionism had its roots in religious Americans called Quakers and a religious movement called the Second Great Awakening. However, the most forceful momentum came from free African Americans con-stantly reminding American

Shortly after his speaking out in support of Lovejoy, Wendell Phillips gave up his law practice and joined the abolitionist movement.

whites of the contradictions in their political philosophy. Americans proclaimed the natural rights of humanity for *all* people, yet had kept the ownership of slaves legal. It had to stop.

Early American Abolitionists

European countries like Britain, Holland, and France all participated in the slave trade. But in the late 1750s, the Quakers began a movement against slavery. Deeply religious, they called themselves The Society of Friends. They hated war, refused to take an oath to anyone or anything, and never took off their hats or bowed to anyone. Because they had been persecuted and driven out of England, the Quakers understood the value of personal choice and freedom of thought.

The first petition against slavery in America was drawn up in Germantown, Pennsylvania—now a part of Philadelphia—in 1688. In their petition, the Quakers explained why they were against slavery:

> There is a saying, that we should do to all men like as we will be done ourselves; making no difference of what generation, descent, or colour [sic] they are . . . To bring men hither [to America], or to rob and sell them against their will, we stand against . . . Pray, what thing in the world can be done worse towards us . . .[1]

Iames Nailor Quaker, fet 2 howers on the Pillory at Wcftminfter, whiped by the Hang man to the old Exchainge London, Som dayes after, Stood too howers more on the Pillory se at the Exchainge, and there had his Tongue Bored throug with a hot Iron, & Stigmatized in the Forehead with the Letter:B: Decemr: 17: anno Dom:1656:

The Quakers had been persecuted in England. Here, Quaker James Naylor (also sometimes spelled Nailor) is whipped and has his tongue burned with a hot iron.

Unfortunately, the Philadelphia Quakers were ignored. It would not be until eighty-six years later in 1774 that the Philadelphia Yearly Meeting of Friends would adopt rules that forbid Quakers to buy or sell slaves. In 1775, the first abolitionist society was founded in Philadelphia—the Pennsylvania Society for the Abolition of Slavery. The antislavery ideas of early white abolitionists were based on two main attitudes: the Golden Rule—doing to others as you would have them do to you—and fear of slave revolts because Quakers believed that the oppression of anyone results in a state of continuous war against those oppressed. Quakers believed that slavery was a sin and ending slavery would purify the world. They also believed that African Americans needed to be helped spiritually before they could be free. These ideas inspired whites who were against slavery. However, blacks did not see the early abolitionist movement in these terms; they felt that slaves should be free simply because it was a basic human right.[2]

In the early years, Quakers were more involved in the abolitionist movement than any other American group. In the nineteenth century, American Quaker women totaled 40 percent of all female abolitionists. Some Quakers believed in the gradual freeing of slaves. Others favored freeing the slaves to live in a colony outside the United States. Others declared that only immediately freeing the slaves in America would suffice. But up to and after the Civil War, the Quakers were at the forefront of the abolitionist movement.[3]

Evangelicalism

American attitudes toward slavery also changed due to the religious feelings sweeping the nation from the 1790s to the 1840s. This religious movement was called the Second Great Awakening. Many people joined the Methodist and Baptist churches, challenging the older and stricter Anglican and Presbyterian faiths. Traveling preachers had the gift of showmanship and converted thousands of people through exciting demonstrations of devotion to God. Evangelical Protestantism had arrived on the scene. Religious control was taken from the established churches, and a relationship grew between political freedom and religious freedom. People started feeling comfortable resisting authority if it meant doing the right thing.[4]

Evangelical religious people, who based their beliefs on "the dignity and equality of humankind," viewed slavery as an outrage because it kept thousands of slaves from learning about the Bible.[5] (There were laws against teaching a slave to read or write, so most slaves were not able to read the Bible.) Evangelicals believed slaves were being held back from personally growing in their religious faith. They also believed that slavery destroyed the morals of the slaveholders, too. But slavery was too deeply rooted in American society. Antislavery ideas were seen as a threat to evangelical churches in the South. Members of these churches were divided when it came to their feelings toward slavery. Many southern churches abandoned the abolitionist cause. As southern proslavery forces defended slavery and stressed their belief in its benefit to the economy, conflict was inevitable. According to historian Donald Mathews, "The social realities of slavery and the psychological realities of racial prejudice simply could not be counterbalanced by religious commitment—they could be affected but not destroyed."[6]

White racism—the belief that the color of a person's skin determines their worth as a human being—among many evangelicals did not prevent the message of the equality of the human spirit from reaching the slaves themselves, however. African Americans adopted evangelical religious beliefs to try and ease their own horrific condition. Evangelicalism opened a new world of escape and created a strong place of connection with white society. Mutual feelings of religious devotion united some church members, black and white.

African-American preachers were emotionally and powerfully expressive. They knew how to move people in meaningful ways. White preachers learned from them. But step by step, even in the face of white opposition, northern blacks founded their own churches and their own brand of evangelicalism. African Americans

PRAYER MEETING

African-American preachers in the North often spoke out against the institution of slavery.

included bits of African folk religion in their sermons along with the promise of deliverance from slavery—like Moses leading the Jewish slaves out of Egypt. Black preachers gave their congregations a sense of independence and empowerment—a feeling of being a chosen people. This message was often carried to slaves in the south via free-black sailors who traveled up and down the East Coast. It helped to ease some of the psychological and spiritual damage of slavery, and kept slaves believing in the moral rightness of freedom.[7]

The Enlightenment and Natural Rights

The natural rights of man—the basis for America's Declaration of Independence—also provided a strong foundation for abolitionism. Founding fathers such as Benjamin Franklin, Thomas Jefferson, and George Washington adhered to these beliefs (even though both Jefferson and Washington were slave owners). These men viewed slavery as immoral, but in a more rational sense. They did not see morality and religion as the same thing. Many religious people believed slavery was good and that slaves should view their owners as "God's overseers."[8]

The first American that examined God and religion also helped inspire the American Revolution. He was a writer named Thomas Paine. In his pamphlet *Rights of Man,* Paine insisted that human rights and liberty were the essence of what it meant to be an independent person—to be fully human. He believed that these rights and liberties should be the same for everyone no matter who they were.[9] But soon after he published *Rights of Man,* Paine saw that religion could enslave people just as easily as kings or dictators. So, he devoted himself to the idea that everyone should understand, from reason alone, that human rights are the very foundation of human life. No one should give them up without a fierce struggle. In 1775, Paine became one of the first Americans to attack the institution of slavery. He wrote an essay entitled "African Slavery in America," which was published just before he became a founding member of the first antislavery society in Philadelphia.

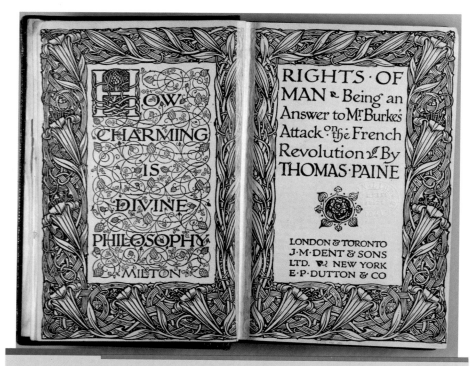

In *Rights of Man*, Thomas Paine outlines the basic rights that he felt a person should have.

African-American slaves quickly understood that the American Revolution could aid them in their search for freedom. Some used a combination of Christianity and the revolutionary principles of liberty and justice to call for their freedom. Others joined the revolutionary army and fought alongside white Americans. This enabled African-American slaves to challenge white Americans' views on slavery. They also hoped that they could earn their freedom by fighting against the British. Still others thought if they fought on the British side and defeated the Americans, they could earn their freedom that way.

The Constitutional Convention

The colonies had already had one fight over slavery in 1776 during the debates over the signing of the Declaration of Independence. But the southern colonies refused to abolish slavery. In order to get the southern representatives to the Constitutional Congress to sign the document, the question of slavery was put off for another day. That day came when the Constitutional Convention was called in 1787. It was time to debate a new constitution for the new country. At this time, slavery was a flourishing business in the United States. Out of about 3.9 million Americans, approximately 700,000 (18 percent) were slaves. In states like Virginia and South Carolina, slaves made up about half the population. Although slavery was mostly in the South, northerners also had slaves—up to thirty thousand in 1789. But, by this time, many people in the North opposed slavery. Vermont banned it in 1777. In the 1780s, Connecticut, Pennsylvania, and Rhode Island started the process of gradual abolition.[10]

George Mason agreed to go to the Convention in Philadelphia during the hot summer of 1787 as one of the delegates from Virginia. He would be one of the fifty-five men from twelve states that would write one of the most important documents in world history. Mason wrote, "the eyes of the United States are turned upon this assembly . . . may God grant that we may be able to gratify them, by establishing a wise and just government."

Throughout the convention, Mason consistently spoke out in favor of individual rights. Agreements were being reached on many major issues that summer, but the discussion on including a bill of rights and abolishing slavery was becoming heated. Even though Mason was a lifelong slave owner, he was for the abolition of slavery. He wrote that "every master of slaves is born a petty tyrant." But Mason was only for abolition as soon as it was economically possible for the people who owned slaves—not immediately. Instead of freeing all slaves that were living in America, Mason desperately wanted to stop all future imports of slaves from Africa. But again, like the debates in 1776, a quick surrender was worked out. The slave trade would continue for another twenty years.[11]

The most infamous provision in the document was the Three-Fifths Clause. This allowed that, since slaves were considered property, they would only be counted as three-fifths of a person when determining the population of a state. This meant that slaves would have no individual rights. Also, a fugitive slave clause was inserted that said that all runaway slaves had to be returned to their owners. All of these laws were put into place without any of the framers using the actual word "slave," which showed their embarrassment that this document of freedom would continue to deny it to others.[12]

George Mason was bitter and angry. He wrote to Jefferson about "the . . . indecent, manner in which the business was conducted, . . . a compromise between the Eastern and the two Southern states to permit the latter to continue the importation of slaves . . . a more

George Washington, who presided over the Constitutional Convention, was a planter and slave owner.

favorite object with them than the liberty and happiness of the people."[13]

Still frustrated by the slavery compromise, George Mason hoped that his proposal to include a bill of rights in the new constitution (he had written one for Virginia in 1776) would be accepted. It was not. On September 12, 1787, Mason's proposal was unanimously defeated. Mason stated he could not support the final version of the Constitution without a "Declaration of Rights."[14] He felt that, without one, there was no protection for the individual against an oppressive government. Even though the Constitution was passed, Mason's and others' objections led to the first ten amendments, known as the Bill of Rights, which were adopted in 1791.

Gabriel's Conspiracy

One who believed wholeheartedly in the idea of freedom was a twenty-four- year-old blacksmith by the name of Gabriel. Owned by Thomas Prosser of Henrico County, Virginia, Gabriel was greatly influenced by the revolutionary debates flowing within Virginia. He decided to strike out for the freedom of the slaves in his state. What came to be known as Gabriel's Conspiracy was a plan to enter Richmond by force, hold the governor hostage, and then bargain for the freedom of every slave in Virginia.

A heavy rainstorm on August 30, 1800, turned the streets of Richmond into a mucky swamp. A few nervous slaves let some whites know of the plan, and

Gabriel's strategy was discovered. Gabriel and his fellow slave conspirators were arrested. At the trial, the man Gabriel asked to speak for him testified that Gabriel intended to "purchase a piece of silk for a flag on which they would have written 'death or liberty.'" Gabriel was referring to a famous Patrick Henry speech in 1775 in which he said "Give me liberty or give me death!" Twenty-seven slaves, including Gabriel, were found guilty and hanged.

Gabriel and his fellow slave conspirators were arrested.

Gabriel's Conspiracy had a great impact on white and black Americans. The rebellion had been widely reported in newspapers throughout the country. During the 1800 presidential campaign, Gabriel's bold idea was used by both political sides. Some Americans said the plan was caused by the support by other Americans for the French Revolution. Overly democratic ideals were the reason why Gabriel took the freedom words so literally. Also, Gabriel's Conspiracy raised already brewing fears of a slave rebellion in the minds of southerners.

The executions bothered some Virginia political leaders. Even James Monroe, the governor that Gabriel had hoped to hold hostage to free the slaves, expressed distress about the number of executions, but pardoning any of them would have been politically out of the question. Thomas Jefferson agreed that "there is a strong sentiment that there has been hanging enough. The other states & the world at large will forever condemn us if we indulge in a principle of revenge."[15]

White witnesses testified that all of the slaves in Gabriel's Conspiracy went to their deaths bravely, with "a sense of their rights and a contempt for danger."[16] A lawyer who was present at their trials said that when one of them was asked what he had to say in his own defense, the slave replied:

> I have nothing more to offer than what General Washington would have had to offer, had he been taken by the British and put to trial by them. I have adventured my life in endeavouring to obtain the liberty of my countrymen, and am a willing sacrifice in their cause: and I beg, as a favour, that I may be immediately led to execution. I know that you have pre-determined to shed my blood, why then all this mockery of a trial?[17]

American Attitudes Toward Slavery

Before the American Revolution, George Washington, like most people of the time, thought that slavery was just a part of life. Society, in the eighteenth century, was made up of many people who lived in various degrees of inequality and bondage, such as women and indentured servants. But slavery was the worst situation for a human being.

Slavery had existed for thousands of years around the world. Every single American colony participated in African slavery in one way or another. Even though southerners owned most of the slaves in the country, slavery was important in the North, too. For example, in the state of New York in the 1740s, 20 percent of the people living there were enslaved.[1] Slavery was a national tradition; it seemed a natural that some people were born into slavery every day. Very few people then thought slavery was wrong or that it needed any explanation or even an apology. Most slaveholders in the South had no feelings of guilt over owning slaves. The eighteenth century was a brutal time, and most life, white and black, was cheap.

The American Revolution changed everything. More people began to question slave ownership. All at once a substantial number of founding fathers saw the obvious contradiction between their calls for liberty and their ownership of slaves. Slavery suddenly became an institution that needed to be defended to continue. However, changes in attitude did not come easy. George Washington struggled to shift from a proslavery to an antislavery attitude. As a boy and young man living in Virginia, he had always accepted a life based on slavery. As a southern planter, Washington was perfectly at home in his southern society. His views on slavery were the same as every other person he knew. But, when Washington became leader of the Continental Army, he encouraged the recruitment of African Americans into the military. He needed fighting men, and did not care how he got them. In 1779, Washington approved a plan to grant slaves their freedom in return for military service. While slaves did serve as soldiers, the plan to offer them their freedom failed because of the deep-rooted racism of American society.[2]

Non-slave-holding northerners, who had generally accepted the institution of slavery before 1776, began to think differently. Slaves were outside the ideal of a free people moving ahead to an industrial future.

Gradually, northerners decided that slavery was bad for the American economy.[3] Northerners saw "free labor," meaning that the workers were free people not slaves, as central to a good society. A successful American society would come from the opportunities made available to the average working man. The dignity of labor was a constant theme in northern politics—paid wages for work was honorable; slavery was not. Many historians trace this idea to the beginnings of American civilization—to the Protestant work ethic where "the pursuit of wealth . . . became a way of serving God." Individual success guaranteed a person's honesty, thrift, persistence, arriving at the job on time, and staying away from alcohol. Being a success in one's work was a sign that God approved.[4]

Southern Beliefs and Economic Development

In the South, African slavery was introduced later in the seventeenth century because the cost of a slave was high compared to indentured servants, who were usually contracted to work for seven years. Growing tobacco in the South was hard work in hot weather, among bugs and snakes. Most people laboring in the

Growing tobacco in the South was hard work in hot weather, among bugs and snakes.

fields died within a few years. To own a slave for life was not good business since that slave could die within a year or two after coming to America. So indentured whites were worked to death instead.[5] As soon as the swamps were cleared along the southern Virginian coast and workers began to live longer, African slavery increased. Lifelong servitude became good business then.

Growing cotton became popular in the 1790s after the invention of the cotton gin by Eli Whitney. Suddenly, southern planters could make cotton profitable because the cotton gin allowed them to grow

PICKING COTTON ON A GEORGIA PLANTATION.

Once cotton became a money-making crop, southern plantation owners enslaved more and more Africans and African Americans.

cotton inland, not just along the coast. The cotton gin was used on an inland variety of cotton that had sticky green seeds. These seeds were difficult to pick out of the fluffy white cotton bolls—it took time if it was being done by hand.[6] The cotton gin separated the seeds from the cotton much more quickly. This invention opened up much more land to be farmed since cotton could be grown in more southern climates. From this time on, the American South became the world's biggest supplier of cotton. This brought the region wealth, growth, and a unity that would hold until the Civil War.[7]

The South became dependent on slave labor because of the enormous success of their cotton crop. Pursuing this type of wealth changed southern society. After the Revolutionary War, southern politicians continually insisted that slavery would never be abolished, because no matter how contradictory slavery was to American ideals—everyone was making money from it. In order to justify the enslavement of people, slaveholders portrayed them as savage, lazy, ignorant, and not equal to whites. For a long time it was against the law to teach the Bible to slaves because southerners felt that slavery and Christianity were incompatible. As early as the late 1660s, slaves would ask for their freedom in the name of Christianity. When slaveholders started making more money, new rules were established that religious conversion would not be tied to freedom. Many white preachers told the slaves that God agreed with their servitude—that they were serving God as slaves.[8]

By 1837, on the floor of the U.S. Senate, Senator John C. Calhoun from South Carolina made a speech against abolition:

> As widely as this incendiary spirit [abolition] has spread, it has not yet infected this body [the Senate] . . . but unless it be speedily stopped, it will spread and . . . [will bring] the two great sections of the Union into deadly conflict . . . but I appeal to all sides whether the South is not equal in virtue, intelligence, patriotism, courage . . . I hold that in the present state of civilization, where two races of different origin, and distinguished by color, and other physical differences, as well as intellectual, are brought together, the relation now existing in the slaveholding States between the two, is, instead of an evil, a good—a positive good.[9]

The Plaindealer in New York criticized Senator Calhoun in an editorial called "The Blessings of Slavery":

> Senator [Calhoun] maintained with much vehemence that slavery is not an evil, but "a good, a great good,". . . his remarks . . . contained some very insulting allusions to the free laborers of the Northern States, whom Mr. Calhoun spoke of . . . as serfs and vassals, far beneath the negro[s] of the South in moral degradation . . . [But] we do hold from the bottom of our soul that slavery is an evil, a deep,

The American Colonization Society

Sending free blacks to Africa was an idea on which both whites and blacks were divided. Some African Americans thought they would never get justice in the United States and supported emigration. Others believed African Americans should remain to fight against slavery and for full legal rights as citizens. Some whites saw colonization as a way to remove all African Americans, especially free blacks, from the United States. They thought that free blacks incited the slaves to rebel. Others believed black Americans would not be discriminated against in Africa, so they would be happier. Many religious Americans thought that African-American colonists in Africa would spread Christianity to the continent.

Formed in 1817, the American Colonization Society sought to send free African Americans to Africa. In 1822, the society established a colony on the west coast of Africa that became the independent nation of Liberia in 1847. But in the 1830s, the society was severely criticized by abolitionists. They proclaimed colonization was just a scheme of the slave owners to rid America of free African Americans. By 1867, the society had sent more than thirteen thousand emigrants. However, after the Civil War, financial support for colonization died down. During its later years, the society focused on educational and missionary efforts in Liberia rather than emigration.[10]

detestable, damnable evil; an evil in all its aspects; an evil to the blacks and a greater evil to the whites; an . . . evil which shows itself in the languishing condition of agriculture at the South, in its paralyzed commerce . . . an evil that stares you in the face . . . and howls in your ears through the tangled recesses of the Southern swamps and morasses.[11]

Northern Beliefs and Economic Development

Many northerners saw the progress of independent farmers and small business owners as very important. Being able to rise above one's economic class was essential. Anyone who worked hard should be able to rise from working for a simple wage to a business owner, according to many people in the North. To many northerners, "free labor" could mean a step up from wage earning to ownership.

As the years went by, the frictions between the believers in "free labor," which celebrated a self-confident middle class, and a rich class of privileged people growing cotton on gigantic plantations using slave labor grew impossible to ignore. Both the North and the South became gradually more isolated from each other—morally and politically. Republicans, a brand new political party in 1854, were suspicious of people who had inherited huge wealth from their families— these people tended to support slavery. Republicans also distrusted the rich people in the eastern cities who wanted to protect their own textile business interests making clothing from the cotton in the South. In Massachusetts, political leaders condemned this partnership between "the lords of the loom and the lords of the lash."[12] Abraham Lincoln, at the time a Republican candidate for president, denounced slavery in 1859 and added "advancement, improvement in condition—is the order of things in a society of equals."

The abolitionists fought slavery on many fronts.

The economies of the North and South would drive forward the feelings about slavery on both sides. The abolitionists were mostly in the North, but not absolutely so. The anti-abolitionists were mostly in the South. The clash between the two philosophies had been a part of the American spirit since the Declaration of Independence and would continue even after the Civil War. The abolitionists fought slavery on many fronts. They needed very brave and powerful activists to achieve their goal of a political union without slavery—not only were they fighting an economic system, but a society built on racism.

The American Anti-Slavery Society

The anti-slavery sentiment in the early 1800s culminated in the formation of the American Anti-Slavery Society. On December 4, 1833, sixty abolitionists from most of the twelve free states in America came

The Abolition of Slavery

He that STEALETH a man, and selleth him, or if he be found in his hand, he shall surely be put to death. —*Ex. xxi. 16.*

Thou shalt not deliver unto his master the servant which is escaped from his master unto thee: He shall dwell with thee, even among you, in that place which he shall choose, in one of thy gates where it liketh him best: thou shalt not oppress him. —*Deut. xxiii. 15, 16.*

And if a man smite the eye of his servant, or the eye of his maid, that it perish, he shall let him go free for his eye's sake. And if he smite out his man-servant's tooth, or his maid-servant's tooth; he shall let him go free for his tooth's sake. —*Ex. xxi. 26, 27.*

If a man be just, and do that which is lawful and right; hath not oppressed any; hath spoiled none by violence; hath executed true judgment between man

and man, &c., shall surely live. —*Ezekiel xviii. 5.—9.*

Is not this the fast that I have chosen? to loose the bands of wickedness, to undo the heavy burdens, to let the OPPRESSED go FREE, and that ye break every yoke. —*Isaiah lviii. 6.*

Ye tithe mint, and anise, and cummin, and all manner of herbs, and pass over the weightier matters of the law, judgment, mercy, and faith: these aught ye to have done, and not leave the other undone. —*Matthew xxiii. 23.*

Thou tread upon the lion and adder; the young lion and the dragon shalt thou trample under feet.

DECLARATION OF THE ANTI-SLAVERY CONVENTION.

ASSEMBLED IN PHILADELPHIA, DECEMBER 4, 1833.

THE Convention assembled in the city of Philadelphia to organize a National Anti-Slavery Society, promptly seize the opportunity to promulgate the following DECLARATION OF SENTIMENTS, as cherished by them in relation to the enslavement of one-sixth portion of the American people.

More than fifty-seven years have elapsed since a band of patriots convened in this place, to devise measures for the deliverance of this country from a foreign yoke. The corner-stone upon which they founded the TEMPLE of FREEDOM was broadly this—"that all men are created equal; that they are endowed by their Creator with certain inalienable rights; that among these are life, LIBERTY, and the pursuit of happiness." At the sound of their trumpet-call, three millions of people rose up as from the sleep of death, and rushed to the strife of blood; deeming it more glorious to die instantly as freemen, than desirable to live one hour as slaves. They were few in number, poor in resources; but the honest conviction that TRUTH, JUSTICE, and RIGHT were on their side, made them invincible.

We have met together for the achievement of an enterprise, without which, that of our fathers is incomplete; and which, for its magnitude, solemnity, and probable results upon the destiny of the world, as far transcends theirs, as moral truth does physical force.

In purity of motive, in earnestness of zeal, in decision of purpose, in intrepidity of action, in steadfastness of faith, in sincerity of spirit, we would not be inferior to them.

Their principles led them to wage war against their oppressors, and to spill human blood like water, in order to be free. Ours forbid the doing of evil that good may come, and lead us to reject, and to entreat the oppressed to reject, the use of all carnal weapons for deliverance from bondage; relying solely upon those which are spiritual, and mighty through God to the pulling down of strong holds.

Their measures were physical resistance—the marshalling in arms—the hostile array—the moral encounter. Ours shall be such only as the opposition of moral purity to moral corruption—the destruction of error by the potency of truth—the overthrow of prejudice by the power of love—and the abolition of slavery by the spirit of repentance.

Their grievances, great as they were, were trifling in comparison with the wrongs and sufferings of those for whom we plead. Our fathers were never slaves—never bought and sold like cattle—never shut out from the light of knowledge and religion—never subjected to the lash of brutal task-masters.

But them, for whose emancipation we are striving—constituting at the present time at least one-sixth part of our countrymen,—are recognised by the law, and treated by their fellow-beings, as marketable commodities—as goods and chattels—as brute beasts; are plundered daily of the fruits of their toil without redress; really enjoying no constitutional nor legal protection from licentious and murderous outrages upon their persons; are ruthlessly torn asunder—the tender babe from the arms of its frantic mother—the heart-broken wife from her weeping husband—at the caprice or pleasure of irresponsible tyrants. For the crime of having a dark complexion, they suffer the pangs of hunger, the infliction of stripes, and the ignominy of brutal servitude. They are kept in heathenish darkness by laws expressly enacted to make their instruction a criminal offence.

These are the prominent circumstances in the condition of more than two millions of our people, the proof of which may be found in thousands of indisputable facts, and in the laws of the slave-holding States.

Hence we maintain—That in view of the civil and religious privileges of this nation, the guilt of its oppression is unequalled by any other on the face of the earth; and, therefore, that it is bound to repent instantly, to undo the heavy burden, to break every yoke, and to let the oppressed go free.

We further maintain—That no man has a right to enslave or imbrute his brother—to hold or acknowledge him, for one moment, as a piece of merchandise—to keep back his hire by fraud—or to brutalize his mind by denying him the means of intellectual, social, and moral improvement.

The right to enjoy liberty is inalienable. To invade it, is to usurp the prerogative of JEHOVAH. Every man has a right to his own body—to the products of his own labour—to the protection of law—and to the common advantages of society. It is piracy to buy or steal a native African, and subject him to servitude. Surely the sin is as great to enslave an AMERICAN as an AFRICAN.

Therefore we believe and affirm—That there is no difference, in principle, between the African slave trade and American slavery:—That every American citizen, who retains a human being in involuntary bondage, as his property, is [according to Scripture] A MAN STEALER:—That the slaves ought instantly to be set free, and brought under the protection of law—That if they had lived from the time of Pharaoh down to the present period, and had been entailed through successive generations, their right to be free could never have been alienated, but their claims would have constantly risen in solemnity—That all those laws which are now in force, admitting the right of slavery, are therefore before God utterly null and void; being an audacious usurpation of the Divine prerogative, a daring infringement on the law of Nature, a base overthrow of the very

foundations of the social compact, a complete extinction of all the relations, endearments, and obligations of mankind, and a presumptuous transgression of all the holy commandments—and that therefore they ought to be instantly abrogated.

We further believe and affirm—That all persons of colour who possess the qualifications which are demanded of others, ought to be admitted forthwith to the enjoyment of the same privileges, and the exercise of the same prerogatives, as others:—That the paths of preferment, of wealth, and of intelligence, should be opened as widely to them as to persons of a white complexion.

We maintain that no compensation should be given to the planters emancipating their slaves—Because it would be a surrender of the great fundamental principle, that man cannot hold property in man—Because SLAVERY is a CRIME, and THEREFORE IT IS NOT AN ARTICLE TO BE SOLD—Because the holders of slaves are not the just proprietors of what they claim; freeing the slaves is not depriving them of property, but restoring it to its right owners; it is not wronging the master, but righting the slave—restoring him to himself—Because immediate and general emancipation would only destroy nominal, not real property; it would not amputate a limb or break a bone of the slaves, but by infusing motives into their breasts would make them doubly valuable to the masters as free labourers; and, because, if compensation is to be given at all, it should be given to the outraged and guiltless slaves, and not to those who have plundered and abused them.

We regard, as delusive, cruel, and dangerous, any scheme of expatriation which pretends to aid, either directly or indirectly, in the emancipation of the slaves, or to be a substitute for the immediate and total abolition of slavery.

We fully and unanimously recognise the sovereignty of each State, to legislate exclusively on the subject of slavery which is tolerated within its limits; we concede that Congress, under the present national compact, has no right to interfere with any of the slave States, in relation to this momentous subject.

But we maintain that Congress has a right, and is solemnly bound to suppress the domestic slave trade between the several States, and to abolish slavery in those portions of our territory which the Constitution has placed under its exclusive jurisdiction.

We also maintain that there are, at the present time, the highest obligations resting upon the people of the free States, to remove slavery by moral and political action, as prescribed in the Constitution of the United States. They are now living under a pledge of their tremendous physical force to fasten the galling fetters of tyranny upon the limbs of millions in the Southern States; they are liable to be called at any moment to suppress a general insurrection of the slaves; they authorize the slave owner to vote for three-fifths of his slaves as property, and thus enable him to perpetuate his oppression; they support a standing army at the South for its protection; and they seize the slave who has escaped into their territories, and send him back to be tortured by an enraged master or a brutal driver. This relation to slavery is criminal and full of danger: IT MUST BE BROKEN UP.

These are our views and principles—these, our designs and measures. With entire confidence in the over-ruling justice of God, we plant ourselves upon the Declaration of our Independence and the truths of Divine Revelation as upon the EVERLASTING ROCK.

We shall organize Anti-Slavery Societies, if possible, in every city, town, and village in our land.

We shall send forth Agents to lift up the voice of remonstrance, of warning, of entreaty, and of rebuke.

We shall circulate, unsparingly and extensively, anti-slavery tracts and periodicals.

We shall enlist the pulpit and the press in the cause of the suffering and the dumb.

We shall aim at a purification of the churches from all participation in the guilt of slavery.

We shall encourage the labour of freemen rather than that of the slaves, by giving a preference to their productions; and

We shall spare no exertions nor means to bring the whole nation to a speedy repentance.

Our trust for victory is solely in GOD. We may be personally defeated, but our principles never. TRUTH, JUSTICE, REASON, HUMANITY, must and will gloriously triumph. Already a host is coming up to the help of the Lord against the mighty, and the prospect before us is full of encouragement.

Submitting this DECLARATION to the candid examination of the people of this country, and of the friends of liberty throughout the world, we hereby affix our signatures to it; pledging ourselves that, under the guidance and by the help of Almighty God, we will do all that in us lies, consistently with this Declaration of our principles, to overthrow the most execrable system of slavery, that has ever been witnessed upon earth—to deliver our land from its deadliest curse—to wipe out the foulest stain which rests upon our national escutcheon—and to secure to the coloured population of the United States all the rights and privileges which belong to them as men, and as Americans—come what may to our persons, our interests, or our reputations—whether we live to witness the triumph of LIBERTY, JUSTICE, and HUMANITY, or perish untimely as martyrs in this great, benevolent, and holy cause. Done in Philadelphia, this Sixth day of December, A. D. 1833.

*Exodus xxi. 16—Deuteronomy xxiv. 7.

Maine.	EFFINGHAM L. CAPRON,	Rhode Island.	New York.	CHALKLEY GILLINGHAM,	JAMES McKIM,
DAVID THURSTON,	JOSHUA COFFIN,		BERIAH GREEN, Jr.	JOHN McCULLOUGH,	AARON VICKERS,
NATHAN WINSLOW,	AMOS A. PHELPS,	JOHN PRENTICE,	LEWIS TAPPAN,	JAMES WHITE.	JAMES LOUGHEAD,
JOSEPH SOUTHWICK,	JOHN G. WHITTIER,	GEORGE W. BENSON,	JOHN RANKIN,		EDWIN P. ATLEE,
JAMES FREDERIC OTIS,	HORACE P. WAKEFIELD,	RAY POTTER.	ABRAM L. COX,	Pennsylvania.	THOMAS WHITSON,
ISAAC WINSLOW.	JAMES G. BARBADOES,		WILLIAM GOODELL,	EVAN LEWIS,	JOHN R. SLEEPER,
New Hampshire.	DAVID T. KIMBALL, Jr.	Connecticut.	ELIZUR WRIGHT, Jr.	EDWIN A. ATLEE,	JOHN SHARP, Jr.
DAVID CAMPBELL.	DANIEL E. JEWETT,		CHARLES W. DENISON,	ROBERT PURVIS,	JAMES MOTT.
Vermont.	JOHN R. CAMBELL,	SAMUEL J. MAY,	JOHN FROST.	JAS. McCRUMMILL,	
ORSON S. MURRAY.	NATHANIEL SOUTHARD,	ALPHEUS KINGSLEY,		THOMAS SHIPLEY,	Ohio.
Massachusetts.	ARNOLD BUFFUM,	EDWIN A. STILLMAN,	New Jersey.	BARTH'W PUSSELL,	JOHN M. STERLING,
DANIEL S. SOUTHMAYD,	WILLIAM L. GARRISON.	SIMEON S JOCELYN,	JONATHAN PARKHURST,	DAVID JONES,	MILTON SUTLIFF,
		ROBERT B. HALL.		ENOCH MACK,	LEVI SUTLIFF.

This declaration of the American Anti-Slavery Society's first convention also lists the names of those who attended, as well as Bible verses that condemn slavery.

to Philadelphia and formed the American Anti-Slavery Society. They drew up and adopted a constitution and dedicated the group to the immediate freeing of the slaves.[13] Membership in this new organization grew quickly, and by 1835 more than four hundred chapters had been created. By 1838, 1,350 chapters were involved in the antislavery movement with more than 250,000 members, black and white, men and women. The main organizers of the American Anti-Slavery Society were William Lloyd Garrison and brothers Arthur and Lewis Tappan.[14]

Every abolitionist attending that day signed William Lloyd Garrison's *Declaration of Sentiments* to drive home their revolutionary message to America. It read in part:

> More than fifty-seven years have elapsed, since a band of patriots convened in this place . . . The corner-stone upon which they founded [America] was broadly this—"that all men are created equal; that they are endowed by their Creator with certain inalienable rights; that among these are life, LIBERTY, and the pursuit of happiness." But those, for whose emancipation we are striving—constituting . . . at least one-sixth part of our countrymen—are recognized by law, and treated . . . as . . . goods . . . as brute beasts [who] are plundered daily of the fruits of their toil without redress . . . at the caprice or pleasure of irresponsible tyrants. For the crime of having a dark complexion, they suffer the pangs of hunger

The Tappan Brothers

American merchants Arthur (1786–1865) and Lewis (1788–1873) Tappan were religious men who became very involved in the fight against slavery. Born in Northampton, Massachusetts, and later inspired by evangelicalism, the brothers became involved with William Lloyd Garrison. In 1833, they helped organize the New York Anti-slavery Society, the American Antislavery Society, and Oberlin College—a school opened to both African Americans and whites. Both Lewis and Arthur frequently stirred up public anger with their abolitionist work. On July 4, 1834, a riot ended with Lewis Tappan's home being ransacked and his furniture burned in the road.

In 1839, the slave ship *Amistad* was taken over by the African captives on board. They wanted the captain to take them back to Africa. Instead, they ended up in America where they were arrested. Lewis Tappan recognized the chance to help the captured Africans and highlight the immorality of slavery. He raised money for the trial and located translators who could speak with the African captives. He also wrote letters to newspapers presenting the Africans' justification for the mutiny and got John Quincy Adams to argue the case before the U.S. Supreme Court. Upon hearing the decision of the Supreme Court, Adams wrote to Tappan, "The captives are free . . . thanks, thanks, in the name of humanity and justice to you."[15]

In 1843, Lewis Tappan visited England and tried to persuade the British government to help end slavery in Texas by lending money to the new territory. In 1846, Lewis helped found the American Missionary Association, and the following year he helped found the *National Era,* which published Harriet Beecher Stowe's *Uncle Tom's Cabin* in 1852.

[and] brutal servitude . . . We shall organize Anti-Slavery Societies . . . in every city, town and village in our land . . .

The *Declaration of Sentiments* further pledged the signers to write and send antislavery books, newspapers, children's literature, and even poetry around the country to convince people that slavery must end. The signers promised to give speeches everywhere they could, and to buy products made by free people rather than slaves. The declaration went on to read:

Submitting this Declaration to the candid examination of the people of this country, and of the friends of liberty throughout the world, we hereby affix our signatures to it; pledging ourselves . . . to overthrow the most execrable system of slavery that has ever been witnessed upon earth; to deliver our land from its deadliest curse; to . . . secure to the colored population of the United States, all the rights and privileges which belong to them as men, and as Americans . . .[16]

The Abolitionists

In 1855, Frederick Douglass wrote an essay describing "Three Kinds of Abolitionists." In this article, Douglass outlined the differences between the Republican Party (also called the Free Soil Party), the Garrisonian Abolitionists, and the Radical Abolitionists.[1]

The Republican Party felt that slavery would fade away if it was not extended outside the South into the new territories. The Garrisonian Abolitionists believed that the Constitution of the United States was a slave document. To work politically against slavery, by voting or joining political parties, was a mistake. The South must be shunned until they came around to the right way of thinking. The Radical Abolitionists broke with the Garrison group and formed their own party—the

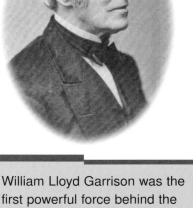

William Lloyd Garrison was the first powerful force behind the abolitionist movement. He started the American Anti-Slavery Society and an antislavery publication called *The Liberator*.

Liberty Party. They believed that the Constitution *did not* allow slavery; all slavery was illegal because the Constitution guaranteed liberty to *all* people. Douglass felt the federal government must abolish all slavery; that an ax had to be applied to the root of the slavery tree. It had to be torn up "root and branch."[2] Eventually, the Radical Abolitionists would split into two groups: those that believed only violence and armed conflict would end slavery and those who chose peaceful means of change.

Frederick Douglass

Frederick Douglass, one of the most famous of the African-American abolitionists, was born on Maryland's eastern shore around 1818. His mother was Harriet Bailey, a slave woman on a plantation owned by Edward Lloyd and his family. There was no birth certificate for her son. In his autobiography, Douglass wrote that he did not know who his father was. Slaves were not issued legal documents for births or marriages. Born a slave, Douglass was considered not much more important than livestock. Since his mother was forced to work on a neighboring farm twelve miles away, she could only visit her son at night. She would finish her work and then walk the long way to see her child. Harriet Bailey called her son her "little Valentine." Later, Douglass would adopt February 14 as his birthday in memory of his mother.[3]

When Douglass was about eight years old, he was sent to live in Baltimore with the Auld family. It changed his life. For the first time, he saw "what I had never seen before; it was a white face beaming with the most kindly emotions; it was the face of my new mistress, Sophia Auld."[4] Even though it was against the law in many states to teach a slave to read and write, Sophia Auld began teaching Douglass to read. It opened up a whole new world to him. As soon as her husband discovered her lessons to Douglass, the reading instruction stopped. Mr. Auld said that teaching a slave to read ". . . would make [the slave] discontented and unhappy." Douglass wrote later,

> These words sank deep into my heart, stirred up sentiments . . . and called into existence an entirely new train of thought . . . I now understood . . . the white man's power to enslave the black man . . . From that moment, I understood the pathway from slavery to freedom . . . Though conscious of the difficulty of learning without a teacher, I set out with high hope, and a fixed purpose, at whatever cost of trouble, to learn how to read.[5]

In his autobiography, Frederick Douglass explained how he paid poor white children who were living nearby with bread to help him learn to read, challenging them to spelling contests on the streets.

Eventually, after much suffering due to a cruel overseer, Douglass escaped from slavery by disguising himself as a sailor and taking a steamship to Philadelphia. He then took a train to New Bedford, Massachusetts.[6] Douglass went to abolitionist meetings there, and loved to read William Lloyd Garrison's newspaper, *The Liberator.* The abolitionist movement against slavery was religious from its earliest beginnings and, by the 1830s, was dominated by the ideas of William Lloyd Garrison, a Boston abolitionist.

A Christian, Garrison believed that slavery was a moral crime and that people who owned slaves could not call themselves Christians. Slavery might be legal, Garrison argued, but it was a sin. To the people that followed Garrison, slavery had to be abolished now—anything else was immoral. This was a new way of seeing the debate over slavery. Most previous antislavery thinkers had stressed a gradual movement away from slavery or moving African Americans out of the country to another homeland. But black and white abolitionists were becoming more united than they ever had been before. No compromises could be made with slavery; it must be ended now.

For a short period, Frederick Douglass lived in England so that he would not be captured and returned to slavery.

Even though Douglass would eventually split with William Lloyd Garrison in a very public way, it was Garrison who first inspired him.[7]

In 1841, Frederick Douglass heard Garrison speak at the Bristol Anti-Slavery Society's annual meeting. At the time, he felt that no one had put into words such a hatred of slavery as Garrison did. Douglass decided to meet him. The twenty-three-year-old Douglass impressed Garrison.

An Independence Day Speech

Frederick Douglass eventually settled in Rochester, New York. He began publishing his own abolitionist newspaper—*The North Star.* Douglass also directed the local Underground Railroad, a secret organization that smuggled escaped slaves into Canada. In 1852, Frederick Douglass was asked to give a speech by the citizens of Rochester to help celebrate the Fourth of July. But in his speech, Douglass delivered a scornful bombardment against the hypocrisy of America. While a nation paraded its freedom and independence with marches and picnics, almost four million human beings were being kept as slaves.

> *The rich inheritance of justice, liberty, prosperity, and independence . . . is shared by you, not by me. The sunlight that brought life and healing to you has brought stripes and death to me . . . Do you mean . . . to mock me, by asking me to speak today? . . . this nation never looked blacker to me than on this Fourth of July . . . Am I to argue that it is wrong to make men brutes, to rob them of their liberty, to work them without wages, . . . to beat them with sticks, to flay their flesh with the lash, to load their limbs with irons, to hunt them with dogs, to sell them at auction, . . . to knock out their teeth, to burn their flesh, to starve them into obedience and submission to their masters? . . . What to the American slave is your Fourth of July? . . . your celebration is a sham . . . a thin veil to cover up crimes which would disgrace a nation of savages. There is not a nation of the earth guilty of practices more shocking and bloody than are the people of these United States at this very hour . . .*[8]

Not long after, Frederick Douglass gave a speech at the Massachusetts Anti-Slavery Society's annual convention in Nantucket. He told the story of his life as a slave. He so moved the audience that one attendee later wrote, "Flinty hearts were pierced, and cold ones melted by his eloquence."[9] That speech launched a career with the American Anti-Slavery Society that would soon inspire millions of Americans and change the course of history.

Sojourner Truth

She was a formidable figure on stage. Almost six feet tall, the woman stood erect with a turban swathed around her head. Her long slim fingers gestured at every point she made as she held the audience spellbound. Sojourner Truth always looked toward tomorrow. She only used the past to tell her story as a slave and as a woman. The future Truth looked to was a world where people of color and women would realize their natural rights, the same rights of all humanity. According to Roseann M. Mandziuk, communications professor at Texas State University and the author of a book on Truth's speeches, Sojourner Truth literally walked away from slavery and she never looked back. "She went out to change the world as she had changed herself, from a person who accepted things the way they were, to a person who knew that she could effect the changes needed to bring about a more perfect union of people."[10]

Sojourner Truth was born in 1797 to parents who were slaves in upstate New York. Her given name was Isabella Baumfree. She had thirteen brothers and sisters.

When she was eleven years old, Isabella was sold away from her family. As a young girl, she was sold several more times and suffered severe hardships. Isabella's third owner, John Dumont, forced her to marry an older slave named Thomas—they had five children. She remained on the Dumont farm because Dumont had promised Isabella her freedom. When he broke his promise, Isabella took her infant child Sophia and ran away to New York City.

In New York, Isabella worked as a housekeeper for wealthy families and for several religious groups. But in 1843, Isabella experienced a spiritual awakening that redirected her life. She changed her name to Sojourner Truth and began preaching throughout the northeast.[11] This new name celebrated the new person she had become—a sojourner dedicated to speaking the truth as revealed by God. She worked and walked her way across Long Island, New York, and then through Connecticut. One religious newspaper reporter described her as ". . . a dignified wanderer in her neat gown and bright bandanna, striding along the sandy roads. Wherever people would listen, she spoke. Where they would take her in, she slept. When they needed help, she stopped to work."[12] All who heard her speak began telling their friends about her. Her fame spread. After months of traveling, she arrived in Northampton, Massachusetts, and joined a utopian community called The Northampton Association for Education and Industry. There, Truth met and worked with abolitionists such as William Lloyd Garrison and Frederick Douglass. Sojourner Truth dictated her memoirs of being a slave and they were

This photo of Sojourner Truth was taken in 1864 as the Civil War raged and the fate of thousands of slaves was being determined.

published in 1850 as *The Narrative of Sojourner Truth: A Northern Slave.*[13]

In 1851, Sojourner Truth helped unite the abolitionist movement to women's rights with her speech before the second annual Ohio Women's Rights Convention in Akron. The editor of a local antislavery paper gave an on-the-scene account:

> One of the most unique and interesting speeches . . . was made by Sojourner Truth, an emancipated slave. It is impossible to transfer it to paper, or convey any adequate idea of the effect it produced upon the audience. Those only can appreciate it who saw her powerful form, her whole-souled, earnest gesture, and listened to her strong and truthful tones. She came forward . . . [and] said with great simplicity: "May I say a few words?" Receiving an affirmative answer, she proceeded.

Sojourner Truth strode to the stage in her usual confident manner. She then proceeded to completely rearrange the abolitionist movement by joining black women and white women together in the effort. Part of what Truth said was:

> I want to say a few words about this matter. I am a woman's rights. I have as much muscle as any man, and can do as much work as any man. I have plowed and reaped and husked and chopped and mowed, and can any man do more than that? I have heard much about the sexes being equal. I can carry as much as any man, and can eat as much too, if I can get it. I am as strong as any man that is now . . .[14]

Sojourner Truth's legacy, as a northern woman, as a powerful speaker, and as an ex-slave, gave American history the story of a person who believed in speaking the truth to everyone who would listen. Sometimes the truth was not very easy for some people to hear. A man in an audience attending an antislavery speech by Sojourner Truth started heckling her. He said, "I don't care any more for your talk than I do for the bite of a flea," Truth answered, "Perhaps not, . . . but the Lord willing I will keep you scratching."[15]

Lucretia Mott

Before 1830, hardly any women were allowed to get up and speak before an audience—until Lucretia Mott. Quaker Lucretia Mott had a favorite saying, "Truth for Authority, not Authority for Truth." People had to have a mind of their own. They should not blindly

Lucretia Mott is considered to be one of the first feminists and the first woman to publicly speak out against slavery.

accept truth merely on governmental authority, religious authority, or even popular opinion. In the 1850s, all these authorities supported slavery in some way. Mott felt that everyone of conscience had to search themselves to find what was true and, once they found out what was true, do their duty.

Born in Nantucket, Massachusetts, in 1793, Lucretia Mott is considered to be one of the first feminists and the first woman to publicly speak out against slavery. Mott was one of the founders of Philadelphia's Female Anti-Slavery Society, and her regal and erect figure became a familiar sight. Mott and her friend Elizabeth Cady Stanton traveled to London to attend the World Anti-Slavery Convention as delegates. Because the two were women, they were not allowed to be seated at the meeting. That treatment inspired Lucretia Mott to work for women's rights as well as abolition. In 1848, Mott and Stanton organized the Women's Rights Convention at Seneca Falls in New York. It was the first women's rights meeting in America.

She was called a "bad woman" and a "female fanatic," but Lucretia Mott continued to tell her truths. At a meeting in Boston, Mott spoke to an audience outlining her creed that many people have taken to heart ever since: "There are signs of progress in the movements of the age . . . it only needs that people examine for themselves—not pin their faith on minister's sleeves, but do their own thinking, obey the truth, and be made free."[16]

A Radical Abolitionist Emerges

A year before Sojourner Truth made her famous speech in Akron, Ohio, Congress passed the Compromise of 1850. This legislation was supposed to bring calm to a nation that was bitterly divided over slavery. The compromise had five key provisions, but three were very important to the slavery question: Popular sovereignty would allow new territories to vote on whether to have slavery; the slave trade was abolished in Washington D.C.; and a new Fugitive Slave Act was passed, requiring that escaped slaves in free states be returned to their owners.[17]

It was not long before the new legislation would be tested. On December 14, 1853, a bill was proposed that would organize the Nebraska territory, which included the area that would become the state of Kansas. Nebraska was north enough and would be a free state, but Kansas was next to Missouri, a slave state. Whether Kansas would be free or slave would be decided by popular sovereignty—the people living there would vote on it. The reaction was explosive. Many northerners, who were Free Soilers, went to the territory to vote for Kansas to be a free state. Southerners, mostly from Missouri, swept over the boundary line to vote proslavery. The powder keg exploded when a group of proslavery men entered the town of Lawrence, burned a hotel, and destroyed printing presses, homes, and stores. A radical abolitionist named John Brown struck back. He led four of his sons and a group of men on an attack at Pottawatomie Creek. Brown dragged five proslavery men from their homes and hacked them to death. After the violence subsided, fifty-five people were dead. This brutal series of events was forever known as "Bleeding Kansas."[18]

John Brown

John Brown's career for the last six weeks of his life was meteor-like, flashing through the darkness in which we live. I know of nothing so miraculous in our history.

—Henry D. Thoreau[19]

John Brown became the most hated man in America, and one of the most adored. Some thought he was crazy. Others thought he was justifiably committed to an important cause. All agreed, though, that John Brown hated slavery with a passion. With his fiery eyes and wild hair, John Brown was quite a sight. When Frederick Douglass spent a night at Brown's house, he was struck by the plainness of the place. He wrote, "It is said that a house in some measure reflects the character of its occupants; this one certainly did. In it there were no disguises, no illusions, no make-believes. Everything implied stern truth, solid purpose, and rigid economy."[20]

John Brown was seen as a saint to some, a terrorist to others.

Brown was born in Connecticut in 1800. Stories told about his life say that he arrived at his deep hatred of slavery when, as a young boy, he witnessed another boy who was a slave, almost beaten to death. As an adult,

Brown would later move his family to North Elba, New York, on lands that wealthy abolitionist Gerrit Smith set aside for an integrated community of blacks and whites to build lives together. Smith and Brown would later trailblaze a transition in the abolitionist movement. Their followers would split from William Lloyd Garrison and the New England Anti-Slavery Party and form a party of more radical abolitionists. In 1840, the Liberty Party was born and it would take the abolitionist movement in a new political direction.[21]

Both black and white abolitionists were getting tired of waiting for southern whites to change their minds about slavery. They wanted to take direct action. The night Frederick Douglass spent at Brown's house was in 1847, and Brown had an idea. Brown wanted to create an armed force of men that would act "in the very heart of the South." He showed Douglass a map of the United States and pointed out the Allegheny Mountains. Brown told Douglass that the Alleghenies were full of "good hiding places" where many men could be concealed who would fight for the freedom of the slaves in Virginia. These men would be supplied with guns and ammunition and could be posted "in squads of fives on a line of twenty-five miles." These fighters would urge slaves to join them and the forces against slavery would grow. Douglass was deeply affected by the passionate ideas of John Brown, although he did not share Brown's desire to resort to violence and would not join in his plan. Later, wondering out loud at an antislavery convention in

Salem, Ohio, Douglass remembered, "I expressed this apprehension that slavery could only be destroyed by blood-shed . . ."[22]

The Raid on Harpers Ferry

The summer of 1859, John Brown took a fake name and rented a farmhouse in Maryland to plan a raid on the United States armory in the town of Harpers Ferry across the Potomac River. Frederick Douglass had warned Brown that he would be walking into a "steel trap" and told him, "you will never get out alive."[23] But on a Sunday night in October, John Brown and twenty-one armed companions, both white and black, overwhelmed the night watchmen at the Baltimore and Ohio Railroad Bridge and a nearby rifle factory. Brown put guards at every place he captured and on the town's street corners. News of Brown's takeover of Harpers Ferry spread quickly, and men from all over Virginia and Maryland were sent to fight Brown and his men.[24] By late Monday morning, John Brown was completely surrounded. Taking cover in a fortified gate-house nearby, Brown rounded up some important townspeople and used them as hostages to get his men to safety. Brown's son attempted to surrender under a white flag, but was shot and killed by a local militia man.[25] By Monday evening, more men arrived—state militias, even the United States Marines. Lieutenant Colonel Robert E. Lee had his orders from President James Buchanan to take command of Harpers Ferry. Lee waited until daybreak to attack Brown and his men.

At dawn, the Marines broke through, killing some of Brown's men with bayonets. Brown was then beaten unconscious. According to Lee's official report, Brown's intention was the liberation of all slaves in Virginia and of the entire South. Robert E. Lee thought the idea was so ridiculous, he assumed John Brown was a madman. Brown and his men had killed three white men and a black railroad worker. Brown had lost ten people, including his two sons.

John Brown was brought to trial the following Thursday, October 20, on charges of treason and murder. The governor of Virginia came to question the

During the battle at Harpers Ferry, John Brown kneels between his two fallen sons.

Dangerfield Newby

Born a slave in 1815, Dangerfield Newby was the first person to die in John Brown's raid on Harpers Ferry. Having been freed by his white father, Newby had a wife and seven children who were still slaves in Virginia. Newby was told by his wife's master that he would free Newby's wife and youngest baby for fifteen hundred dollars. Unbelievably, Dangerfield was able to get this large amount of money. He went back to buy his wife and child's freedom. But the slave owner decided to raise the price for Newby's family at the last moment. The new request for money was achingly out of reach. The desperate father decided to join John Brown, hoping to eventually free his whole family.[26]

A letter was found on Dangerfield Newby's body after he was killed. It read in part:

> Dear Husband: I want you to buy me as soon as possible, for if you do not get me somebody else will . . . the last two years have been like a troubled dream to me. It is said Master is in want of money. If so, I know not what time he may sell me, and then all my bright hopes of the future are blasted, for there has been one bright hope to cheer me in all my troubles, that is to be with you . . . Do all you can for me, which I have no doubt you will. I want to see you so much.[27]

Dangerfield Newby was shot in the throat, killing him instantly. Newby was then stabbed repeatedly, and his body mutilated.[28] The body of one of John Brown's sons, Oliver, was placed in the lifeless arms of Dangerfield Newby as a joke, and then Oliver and Newby were dumped into an unmarked grave on the banks of the Shenandoah River.[29] Newby's wife and children were sold farther into the Deep South after the raid on Harpers Ferry.

prisoner and brought reporters with him who helped spread the story of John Brown and his raid on Harpers Ferry. Brown became instantly famous. Word spread that weapons had been found at the farmhouse where Brown and his men had stayed. A large bag was also found packed full of letters from Brown's well-known abolitionist supporters—important people in the North that had financed his raid. The people of the South were angry and became afraid that the entire North approved of the attack.

The trial hardly took any time. Brown's lawyer wanted to have him declared insane, but Brown refused. On November 2, a jury found John Brown guilty of murder, treason, and inciting slaves to rise up against their masters. Before he was sentenced, Brown stood and spoke an address to the court, ending with the words:

> Now, if it is deemed necessary that I should forfeit my life, for the furtherance of the ends of justice, and MINGLE MY BLOOD FURTHER WITH THE BLOOD OF MY CHILDREN, and with the blood of millions in this Slave country, whose rights are disregarded by wicked, cruel, and unjust enactments,—I say LET IT BE DONE.[30]

Brown was sentenced to be executed by hanging. Giving in to Southern fears that supporters in the North would try and rescue Brown, the governor of Virginia ordered over one thousand troops to guard the prisoner. Brown was hanged at midday on December 2, 1859.[31]

Antislavery Views in Print

A number of individuals have established an association . . . for the purpose of effecting the immediate abolition of Slavery . . . One of the means . . . has been the printing of a large mass of newspapers, pamphlets, tracts, and almanacs, containing exaggerated, and in some instances, false accounts of the treatment of slaves, illustrated . . . to operate on the passions of the colored men, and produce discontent, assassination, and servile war. These they attempted to disseminate throughout the slaveholding States, by the agency of the public mails. . . . The position assumed by this Department, is . . . withholding its agency, generally, in giving circulation to the obnoxious papers in the Southern States.

—Postmaster General Amos Kendall, 1835[1]

Amos Kendall, President Andrew Jackson's postmaster general, believed if antislavery materials were delivered in the South, it would incite rebellion and threaten domestic security. Therefore, he advised against circulating "the obnoxious papers." That same year, President Jackson addressed Congress about the post office and freedom of the press. Tensions between the North and South were growing to dangerous levels. Many southern politicians and local postmasters were urging a ban on what they thought were treasonous newspapers, magazines, and newsletters. What they really were upset about was abolitionist material that portrayed southern slave owners as evil and brutal to their slaves. To many in the South, being against slavery meant being a traitor. Jackson, a southerner, strongly suggested that Congress pass a law to allow the ban, but the bill was defeated in the Senate. According to the federal government, it was legal for antislavery literature to be mailed. But, many state governments in the South passed laws restricting these texts. So, postmasters in the South had to break a federal law to obey a state law, or break a state law to obey a federal law.[2]

This was not the first time that the supporters of slavery wanted to stop discussions of ending slavery or suppress speech on the effect slavery was having on the country. A few years before, with membership in the American Anti-Slavery Society exploding, legislators in the House of Representatives were being sent antislavery petitions by the thousands. This was due to a petition drive from the abolitionists—in 1837 and 1838 alone citizens sent over 130,000 petitions to Congress. To end the debate over the abolitionist petitions, the House passed gag rules in 1836 that set the petitions aside, effectively stopping any deliberation.[3] Then, the brilliant representative from Massachusetts, John Quincy Adams, stepped into the fight in 1837. (Adams was a former president of the United States and would later help defend the slaves from the ship *Amistad*.) Even though the battle lasted eight years, Adams eventually won to have the gag rules repealed.[4]

Why were the slave owners and the people who supported them so afraid of newspapers like *The Liberator* by William Lloyd Garrison, *The North Star* by Frederick Douglass, or *The St. Louis Observer* by Elijah Lovejoy? Because the press is very important to the success of any idea. The French emperor Napoleon Bonaparte once said, "Four hostile newspapers are more to be dreaded than one hundred thousand bayonets."[5] Just the mere fact that the southern slave owners tried everything in their power to stop the abolitionist press illustrates how afraid of it they truly were. Many antislavery newspapers, like Benjamin Lundy's *Genius of Universal Emancipation* in 1821, promoted the colonization of slaves outside the United States.

Five years later, antislavery papers began appearing quickly, one after the other. *The African Observer* was published in 1826 in Philadelphia; in 1827, *Freedom's Journal,* the first African-American newspaper, began in New York City; Boston's *National Philanthropist* was established; then *The Investigator* in Providence, Rhode Island; and in 1828, the *Free Press* in Vermont and the *Liberalist* in New Orleans began publishing. With the arrival of the popular *The Liberator,* the free states blossomed with similar papers dedicated to the overthrow of slavery. By 1838, it was estimated that the number of abolitionist publications being distributed was over a hundred.[6]

The Liberator

The Liberator first debuted January 1, 1831, with William Lloyd Garrison's famous opening essay on his determination to fight slavery, "I will be as harsh as truth, and as uncompromising as justice. On this subject I do not wish to think, or speak, or write, with moderation. . . . I am in earnest—I will not equivocate—I will not excuse—I will not retreat a single inch—AND I WILL BE HEARD."[7] Immediately after the publication of the paper "Garrisonian" societies started popping up. By the end of the year, Garrison noted that *The Liberator* was the center of a swelling network of abolitionist societies throughout the northeastern states. Almost everyone who was interested in freeing slaves was reading it.

The Liberator engaged debate on every significant subject or argument within the abolitionist movement. Should the freeing of the slaves be gradual or immediate? Should abolitionists work with southern politicians to end slavery or should they demand an immediate end to slavery without compromise? Should women remain behind the scenes or move into a nontraditional role and speak out themselves? How should the various antislavery groups bring together the different religious beliefs concerning slavery?[8] After a shaky start, William Lloyd Garrison and *The Liberator* led a tireless campaign on behalf of women's rights. *The Liberator* often portrayed

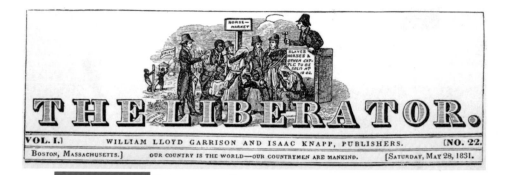

Pictured is the masthead of *The Liberator*. A newspaper's masthead includes the newspaper name, date, issue number, and other identifying information.

the clergy as "kingpins in a conspiracy to oppress women. Reprinting incendiary articles that declared women unfit for the pulpit, and supplementing those with its own strident demands for equality."[9]

Most of the radical abolitionist leaders had been inspired by *The Liberator* and were early readers because of the paper's uncompromising stance toward slavery—it was a sin and must end. No political compromise with the South would be made. Many of these readers also eventually wrote for the publication. The newspaper featured articles stressing the cruelties of slavery and the injustices inflicted on African Americans. As the tensions escalated on the run-up to the Civil War, *The Liberator* would reprint the fiery speeches made on the floors of the Senate and House of Representatives to influence northern public opinion.[10]

An Antislavery Story

Antislavery pamphlets and leaflets contained poems, essays, sermons, and songs. Abolitionists also wanted to influence future generations to continue the fight against slavery, if they were unable to succeed. They created children's literature to tell the tale of the brutality of slavery to a young audience and extend their ideas of freedom more widely.

The book *Little Laura, the Kentucky Abolitionist* was written by an unknown British author and was published in 1859. It was closely associated with the Peace Society led by an American abolitionist named Elihu Burritt. It is believed that the "Laura" in the story was the real-life daughter of a Kentucky abolitionist newspaperman, William Bailey. Southern sympathizers were so angered by the newspapers William Bailey was putting out that, just like Elijah Lovejoy, they burned his printing presses.

In the story, Laura is shunned by some of her classmates. The classmates' parents call Laura the "Abolitionist." But other children gathered around her at recess to ask questions and hear her tell stories of the poor slaves "whose children would often steal into the group under the shade of trees where they sat to hear her answers."[11] The story continues about Laura's sweetness of heart, and that being called "the Abolition girl" in a mean way did not prevent her from speaking out against slavery. Working alongside her father setting type for the printing press to further the cause of freedom, Laura becomes ill and eventually dies at the age of ten.

The North Star

Frederick Douglass' newspaper, *The North Star,* was named for the celestial star that slaves often followed to reach the North and freedom. Debuting in 1847, the newspaper was dedicated to all African Americans, both slave and free. Douglass wrote, "What you suffer, we suffer; what you endure, we endure. We are indissolubly united, and must fall or flourish together."[12] Douglass was committed to abolitionism, black success and equality, and women's rights. These reforms went before all other social concerns. At the top of the front page of

Articles in this issue of *The North Star* discussed the evils of slavery.

An Anti-Slavery Song

Anti-slavery songs were also very popular for the young and old. When well-known patriotic songs were used to spread abolitionist ideas, it especially angered the supporters of slavery. Two stanzas of this song are sung to the melody of "My Country 'Tis of Thee." It was featured in *Anti-Slavery Melodies: For the Friends of Freedom* published for The Hingham Anti-Slavery Society in 1843.

My country! 'tis of thee
Stronghold of slavery,
Of thee I sing:
Land where my fathers died,
Where men man's rights deride,
From every mountainside,
Thy deeds shall ring.

My native country! thee,
Where all men are born free,
If white their skin:
I love thy hills and dales,
Thy mounts and pleasant vales,
But hate thy negro sales,
As foulest sin.[13]

every issue were the words: "Right is of no sex; truth is of no color, God is the Father of us all—and all are brethren."[14] Douglass' passions revolved around civil rights for all, in addition to a belief that a society must help every one of its people to achieve their personal best. His motivation and logic was inspired by his search for "morality, order, and progress." In the first edition of *The North Star*, Douglass wrote that "while our paper shall be mainly Anti-Slavery, its columns shall be freely opened to the candid and decorous discussion of all measures and topics of a moral and humane character, which may serve to enlighten, improve, and elevate mankind."[15]

Unlike the Garrisonians, Douglass began saying that political action could be arguably used against the supporters of slavery. In the February 9, 1849, issue of *The North Star,* Douglass answered a man who wanted to debate him, saying that the Constitution was an antislavery document. In short, Douglass wondered why the debate should take place because he agreed with him. He wrote, "Resolved, That the Constitution of the United States, if strictly construed according to its reading, is antislavery in all of its provisions." Douglass had moved from the strict Garrisonian reading of the Constitution as completely proslavery to a different view—one that could keep the country intact if Americans could agree that slavery was inconsistent with a clear reading of the Constitution.[16] Eventually, he changed the name of *The North Star* to the *Frederick Douglass' Paper* (1851–1959), then to the *Douglass' Monthly* (1859–1863), and finally to the *New National Era* (1870–1873).

The Underground Railroad

The Underground Railroad was a spontaneous, but organized, system for helping fugitive slaves escape to safety in Canada or to northern free states. The name, Underground Railroad, was first used in the early 1840s. As time went on, more symbolic railroad expressions were added. Runaway slaves were called "passengers." The homes that hid the fugitive slaves were "stations." People who led the runaway slaves to freedom were "conductors." Most of the aid given to slaves on their way north was by northern abolitionists, both black and white. But people who were not officially connected to the Underground Railroad also impulsively gave a lot of the help. Some people instantly sympathized with the frightened travelers as soon as they met them, and offered a helping hand.

Free African Americans, like Harriet Tubman, played a major role in the Underground Railroad. They helped slaves on plantations make their daring way North through the most dangerous leg of the journey—

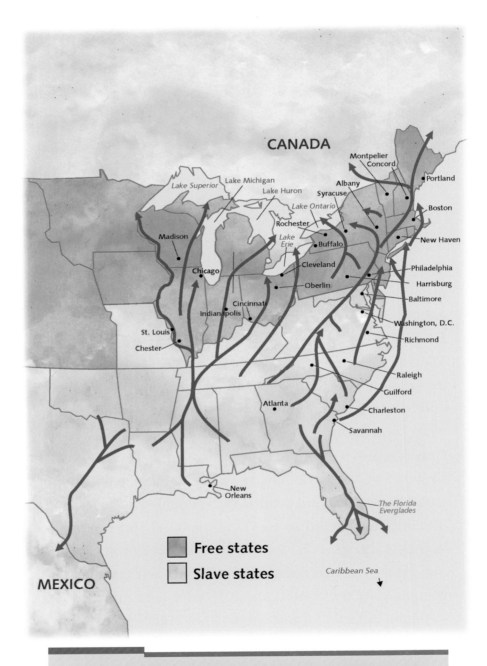

Most routes of the Underground Railroad led to the northern states or to Canada.

the southern routes. In some urban areas—such as Philadelphia, Pennsylvania; Cincinnati, Ohio; and Wilmington, Delaware—Quakers were prominent as conductors. But some scholars have found it extremely hard to separate fact from fiction in the tales of the Underground Railroad. Between 1840 and 1860, a few thousand African-American slaves were able to escape successfully. Most runaways, though, never made it out of the South. Interestingly, instead of keeping the escape stories secret, details of the perilous stories were told everywhere in print and discussed in churches and pubs. The abolitionists used the tales of the dramatic

Conductors of the Underground Railroad help an escaped slave as slave hunters in the background keep a watchful eye.

Underground Railroad to illustrate the evils of slavery. Southern slaveholders and their supporters publicized the escapes to show that northerners were not complying with the fugitive slave laws.[1] Most of the stories of the Underground Railroad were true and brought desperate people to safety, but there were also folktales that were passed from one person to another.[2] In this instance, both truth and fiction inspired people to help one another and many were saved.

Levi Coffin

Levi Coffin, often called "The President of the Underground Railroad," was born into a Quaker family in 1789 in New Garden, North Carolina. Even though Coffin was raised in a slave state, his parents taught him Quaker beliefs. These beliefs created strong antislavery ideas in the young man. Even though he had very little formal schooling, Coffin started a Sunday school for local slaves and African Americans who were free. But local whites soon shut it down. Whites were not supposed to teach the Bible to slaves at that time, or teach slaves to read and write. In 1826, Coffin moved to what is now Fountain City in the state of Indiana and

Levi Coffin helped roughly three thousand slaves to freedom.

opened a store. Almost immediately, Coffin realized that the town was directly on the route of the Underground Railroad. He wanted to help. So, for the next twenty years, Coffin was one of the primary conductors of fugitive slaves to Canada through the Midwest. His house became the famous station where the woman whom Harriet Beecher Stowe would base her character "Eliza" on from her famous book *Uncle Tom's Cabin* passed through on her way to freedom.[3]

Coffin remembered the moment he first understood that slavery was wrong. He was seven years old when a particular incident occurred. He wrote about it later in the story of his life: "It made a deep and lasting impression on my mind." Coffin recalled that, as a boy, he lived for a time in one of the states that supplied the southern slave market—Virginia and Maryland. Free blacks would be kidnapped in Pennsylvania and then sent to these states to be hurried along to Georgia, Alabama, and Louisiana to be sold. The group of kidnapped slaves would be marched through his town:

> The gangs were handcuffed and chained together, and driven by a man on horseback . . . One day I was by the roadside where my father was chopping wood . . . [the] slaves came first, chained in couples on each side of a long chain which extended between them . . . My father addressed the slaves pleasantly, and then asked: "Well, boys, why do they chain you?" One of the men, whose . . . expression denoted the deepest sadness, replied: "They have taken us away from our wives and children, and they chain us lest we should make

our escape and go back to them.". . . I turned to my father and asked many questions . . . why they were taken away from their families . . . In simple words, suited to my comprehension, my father explained to me the meaning of slavery, and, as I listened, the thought arose in my mind—"How terribly we should feel if father were taken away from us."[4]

Harriet Tubman

The fiery and unconquerable Harriet Tubman made a vow when she finally got to freedom:

I looked at my hands, to see if I was the same person now [that] I was free. There was such a glory over everything, the sun came like gold through the trees, and over the fields, and I felt like I was in heaven . . . I had crossed the line of which I had so long been dreaming. I was free; but there was no one to welcome me to the land of freedom, I was a stranger in a strange land, and my home after all was down in the old cabin quarter, with the old folks, and my brothers and sisters. But to this solemn resolution I came; I was free, and they should be free also; I would make a home for them in the North, and the Lord helping me, I would bring them all there.[5]

Harriet Tubman was born a slave on Maryland's Eastern Shore around 1821, and worked as a slave until she was twenty-eight years old. Like most slaves living in the upper southern states, Tubman was deathly afraid of being sold to the Deep South. Places like Georgia,

Harriet Tubman (1823 – 1913)
nurse, spy and scout

During the Civil War, Harriet Tubman worked as a spy for the Union Army during her many trips to the South.

Alabama, and Louisiana were worse places to be a slave than Maryland or Delaware. The plantations were full of swamps. The weather was hot and unbearable to work in. Most slaves knew that once you were in the Deep South, escape was almost impossible. It was an isolated and treacherous country. In 1849, Tubman found out she was going to be sold. So, Tubman did what other runaway slaves did, according to historian Deborah Gray White in her essay "Let My People Go: 1804–1860"— Tubman "joined the thousands of others who took to the woods and stole themselves."[6] Since slaves were legally

In this painting by Paul Collins, Harriet Tubman leads a group of African Americans to freedom.

the property of others, when they ran away, it was called "stealing yourself."

Tubman took dangerous chances. Unlike other escaped slaves, after Tubman had reached safety, she kept returning to the South again and again to rescue her family—her parents, her sisters and brothers, and her sister's children. People began calling Harriet Tubman "Moses" in honor of the fact that she acted much like the biblical leader of the Israelites who led the Jews out of Egypt. She returned to the slave states nineteen times and rescued over three hundred slaves. Maryland slave owners were so angered by her success that there was a forty thousand dollar bounty on her head. If anyone captured Harriet dead or alive, they would get the money.[7]

Harriet Tubman figured out clever ways that helped make her part of the Underground Railroad a success. Sometimes she would use a plantation owner's horse and buggy for the first part of the passage to freedom to escape detection. Riding in a slave owner's buggy kept others from being suspicious. Conductor Tubman and her passengers would leave on a Saturday night, since notices that a slave had run away could not be published in the newspapers until Monday morning. If she met any possible slave hunters, Tubman would turn the buggy onto a road going south to fool them. One time, she met some white men who were reading her "wanted" poster offering the money for her capture. The poster said she could not read, so she tricked them by pulling a book out and pretending to read it. Harriet Tubman even carried a gun, and would warn her passengers that, if they became too tired or wanted to turn back, she'd absolutely use it. Tubman said, "You'll be free or die."[8]

William Still

Philadelphian William Still has been called the "Father of the Underground Railroad." He was one of the most important conductors because he carefully recorded every passenger's name and their circumstances by interviewing the fugitive slaves he helped escape to Canada. What Still wrote is the only nearly complete record of the operations of the Underground Railroad that has been saved. He risked being put in prison for his work with the Philadelphia Vigilance Committee, a group of people that aided hundreds of runaways. According to the Fugitive Slave law, William Still could suffer severely for preserving these records, but he did it anyway. From his own personal history, William Still knew that the names, detailed relationships, and locations of the escaping people were important. With this information, people could have a hope of finding their family if they themselves were freed from slavery. Everyone would know their history, too. William Still hid his notes in a loft at a nearby school and in a local graveyard. In 1873,

William Still

THE

UNDERGROUND RAIL ROAD.

A RECORD

OF

FACTS, AUTHENTIC NARRATIVES, LETTERS, &C.,

Narrating the Hardships Hair-breadth Escapes and Death Struggles

OF THE

Slaves in their efforts for Freedom,

AS RELATED

BY THEMSELVES AND OTHERS, OR WITNESSED BY THE AUTHOR;

TOGETHER WITH

SKETCHES OF SOME OF THE LARGEST STOCKHOLDERS, AND
MOST LIBERAL AIDERS AND ADVISERS,
OF THE ROAD.

BY

WILLIAM STILL,

For many years connected with the Anti-Slavery Office in Philadelphia, and Chairman
of the Acting Vigilant Committee of the Philadelphia Branch of
the Underground Rail Road.

Illustrated with 70 fine Engravings by Bensell, Schell and others, and
Portraits from Photographs from Life.

Thou shalt not deliver unto his master the servant that has escaped from his master unto thee.—*Deut.* xxiii. 15.

SOLD ONLY BY SUBSCRIPTION.

PHILADELPHIA:
PORTER & COATES,
822, CHESTNUT STREET.
1872.

The title page of William Still's *The Underground Railroad*, published in 1872 he published his best material in a book *The Underground Railroad*. Still's illustrated anthology is a succession of "profiles in courage of the men, women and children who passed through his station."[9]

Born October 7, 1821, William Still grew up poor on a farm in the Pine Barrens of New Jersey near the town of Medford. He was the youngest in a family of eighteen children born to parents who had been slaves. His father had purchased his own freedom from a Maryland farmer, but his mother Sidney had to escape. On the second try, she was finally able to join her husband and changed her name to Charity to hide her identity from the slave hunters.

William Still grew up with an intense desire to learn. Armed with no more than a few hours of formal education a year, Still devoured every book he could. His parent's life history and courage was inspiring to him so he decided to devote his life and work to helping the African-American community surrounding him. In 1844, William moved to Philadelphia; he worked for a wealthy widow, waited on tables, and worked in a brickyard. But in 1847, Still applied for a job as a clerk at the Pennsylvania Anti-Slavery Society. It changed his life. For the next fourteen years, serving as the clerk and corresponding secretary, William Still evolved into one of the most important agents for the Underground Railroad. It was a dangerous job because professional slave hunters were always seeking fugitive slaves throughout the streets of Philadelphia. Still secretly hid runaways in his own home at 832 South Street and

Henry "Box" Brown

Henry Brown was angry. His master refused to buy his wife from another owner who was selling her to a slave dealer—then to the Deep South. For five months, Henry Brown had mourned for her and burned with hatred for his master. Brown's owner had made lots of money from Brown's work as a tobacconist in Richmond, Virginia. Feeling betrayed, he decided to make one of the greatest escapes in American history.

"One day, while I was at work, and my thoughts were eagerly feasting upon the idea of freedom . . . the idea suddenly flashed across my mind of shutting myself *up in a box,* and getting myself conveyed as dry goods to a free state."

Henry Brown found a carpenter to build the box. They addressed the box to a friend in Philadelphia. Brown bored three holes for air and stashed a container of water in the box. His friends nailed down the lid and took him to the Express Office. "I had no sooner arrived at the office than I was turned heels up."

Brown was later put on board a boat, and "I was again placed with my head down, and in this dreadful position had to remain for nearly an hour and a half." From wagon to steamboat to train, Brown spent twenty-seven hours in that box, much of the time upside down. Finally, he was placed in a depot in Philadelphia with the other luggage. He was weak and worried. Then, he heard a voice asking about his box. He was placed on a wagon and finally transported to a safe house. It was a station on the Underground Railroad, and one of the conductors was William Still. Henry Brown later wrote:

> A number of persons soon collected round the box after it was taken into the house, but as I did not know what was going on I kept myself quiet. I heard a man say "let us rap upon the box and see if he is alive;" . . . and a voice said, tremblingly, "Is all right within?" to which I replied—"all right." The joy of the friends was very great; when they heard that I was alive they soon managed to break open the box, and then came my resurrection from the grave of slavery.[10]

at the home of his Quaker friend Samuel Johnson in Germantown, Philadelphia—many times with the help of Harriet Tubman.

Still helped several of John Brown's supporters who wanted to buy guns for a nationwide slave revolt.

Still was an important figure in the famous escape of Henry "Box" Brown. William Still opened the crate Brown had shipped himself in by overland express from Richmond, Virginia, to Philadelphia. After the raid on the arsenal at Harpers Ferry in 1859, Still helped several of John Brown's supporters who wanted to buy guns for a nationwide slave revolt. John Brown's daughter, Annie, sent William Still a strand of John Brown's hair. It was clipped from Brown's head the day after he was hanged. Along with the hair and locket came a note from Annie: "Mother sends a lock of father's hair which she promised you. She also sends her love to you and your family."[11]

William Still was a born historian. If it had not been for his intrepid spirit and meticulous recordkeeping, much of the day-in and day-out operations of the Underground Railroad would be unknown today. Still's descendants still reside in New Jersey and are active in promoting his civil rights legacy and his life.

A Long Fight

In 1835, the American Anti-Slavery Society increased its publication of abolitionist pamphlets significantly from about one hundred thousand pieces to one million. Over twenty thousand fliers, periodicals, and newsletters were mailed to southern towns while lecturers, black and white, traveled all over the North giving speeches. The South responded with anger, panic, and then violence.

The Nat Turner Rebellion, a slave insurrection that had resulted in the deaths of fifty-five white slave owners, had occurred just a few years earlier. This had increased southern fears. Many southerners thought that the abolitionist literature was inciting similar types of violence. Southern plantation owners worried it might stir up their slaves to rebel, too, so rewards for important abolitionist leaders were offered for their capture dead or alive. Local town elders organized vigilante groups to police free black neighborhoods. They used patrol boats to watch the coastal waterways for runaway slaves. Post offices were searched for any abolitionist material. In Charleston, South Carolina, mobs broke into a post office and publicly burned mail from abolitionists. Even some people in the North were starting to disapprove of abolitionists.[1] Racism was not restricted to the South, by any means.

Prudence Crandall was a Quaker and a teacher who decided to open a private school for girls in Canterbury, Connecticut, in 1831. Soon after, the school was acclaimed as one of the best in the state. But early in 1833, a young African-American girl was admitted to the school and the town immediately and loudly protested. Crandall contacted William Lloyd Garrison. She wanted advice. She got some, and in March 1833, she opened a new school for "young ladies and little misses of color" on the same plot of land as her private school. The local people were outraged. They perse-cuted Crandall and within a few weeks Connecticut lawmakers passed a bill forbidding the organization of schools for African Americans who were not state residents. Publicity followed and many famous abolition-ists came to Crandall's aid, but she was arrested and convicted under the "Black Law" and jailed until July 1834. Local mobs turned violent and eventually burned the school to the ground.[2]

Prudence Crandall

In the first half of the ninteenth century, Anti-African-American and anti-abolitionist riots broke out in St. Louis, Pittsburgh, Cincinnati, and even Quaker Philadelphia. Antislavery meetings were continuously broken up by angry mobs throughout the 1830s and 1840s.

Eventually slavery became the largest source of anger in party politics. With the expansion of the country into the West, many people believed in the idea of Manifest Destiny—a belief that the United States should conquer the entire continent for whites. Many northerners started questioning if slavery should expand, too. Southern slaveholders believed their future depended on the extension of slavery in order to keep political power in the Senate. They were proud that slavery had grown halfway across the country from the eastern coast to New Mexico. Southerners felt that northern objections to slavery were an insult to the morals of southerners. Northerners were becoming a barrier to the South's economic prosperity—the South argued that they had a right to carry their property (slaves) wherever they wanted to move.

By 1850, there were four hardened political positions on slavery: (1) ban all slavery in the new territories, (2) Congress had no right to regulate slavery in the new territories, (3) extend the Missouri Compromise line of 1820 to the Pacific Ocean, and (4) let the settlers decide for themselves if slavery would be in their territory. Pandemonium over the slavery question broke out among the legislators in

$100 REWARD!

RANAWAY

From the undersigned, living on Current River, about twelve miles above Doniphan, in Ripley County, Mo., on 2nd of March, 1860, **A NE GRO MAN,** about 30 years old, weighs about 160 pounds; high forehead, with a scar on it; had on brown pants and coat very much worn, and an old black wool hat; shoes size No. 11.

The above reward will be given to any person who may apprehend this said negro out of the State; and fifty dollars if apprehended in this State outside of Ripley county, or $25 if taken in Ripley county.

APOS TUCKER.

This poster offers a reward for a runaway slave.

Washington, D.C., with fistfights in the halls and representatives challenging each other to duels to the death. In 1850, a compromise was eventually worked out that banned the slave trade in Washington, D.C., and decreed that people living in the new territories would vote on the slavery question. But a particular passage provoked a political uproar and recharged the abolitionist movement—The Fugitive Slave Act.[3]

The Fugitive Slave Act took runaway slave cases away from the courts in the North and gave the cases to federal officials. These officials were to be paid ten dollars if they decided that an African-American captive should be returned to slavery, but only five dollars if they ruled

that the black captive was free. Abolitionists were outraged. They said that this difference in pay would
encourage the commissioners to send everyone south
to slavery.

Harriet Beecher Stowe was furious and she decided
to write about it. The result was her book *Uncle Tom's
Cabin*. The book put before the American public the
anguish and pain of runaway slaves, and it turned
American sentiment against slavery and the Fugitive
Slave Act. *Uncle Tom's Cabin* was published on March
20, 1852. Even though it was not the first antislavery
novel, it was the most
famous and successful.
Uncle Tom's Cabin sold
ten thousand copies in the
first week and three hun-
dred thousand by the end
of the first year. Within
two years, two million
copies had been sold
worldwide. The book was
popular because it made
white readers realize that
African Americans had
deep feelings just like
whites did. A play was
written that was based on
the novel and audiences
flocked to see it. People
both loved and criticized

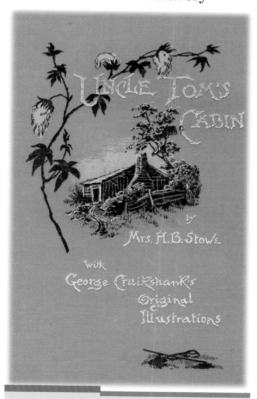

The front cover of Harriet Beecher
Stowe's *Uncle Tom's Cabin*.

Harriet Beecher Stowe

Harriet Elisabeth Beecher was born on June 14, 1811, in Connecticut. She had eleven brothers and sisters and her father, the Reverend Lyman Beecher, was an important and very influential minister. Beecher's mother, Roxanna, died when she was only five years old, but her mother prized education. Harriet was brought up to pursue her dreams. In those days, many people believed that it was wasteful to educate women, that they should only learn housework—not the Beechers. Reverend Beecher was an abolitionist who preached sermons against slavery and his commitment had a deep impact on every one of his children. The family would have lively debates almost every day on important political issues of the day.

In 1832, Harriet moved with her family to Cincinnati, Ohio. Cincinnati was thought of as part of the frontier then, as the country was expanding westward. Harriet met and married Calvin E. Stowe, a professor, and they had seven children. Being a busy mother did not shield Harriet Beecher Stowe from the realities of her world. Cincinnati was just across the river from a slave state—Kentucky. Harriet started to understand the true horror of slavery. One day, she discovered that her paid servant, Zillah, was really a runaway slave. They drove her immediately to a station on the Underground Railroad. Not long after this incident, Harriet was talking to a friend and he told her a story. He saw a young woman desperately running across the icy Ohio River trying to escape to freedom with her baby clutched in her arms. This story so inspired Harriet Beecher Stowe that it became the famous scene of Eliza leaping across the ice, clinging to her daughter, as she is chased by the howling dogs of the cruel slave dealer Simon Legree. It was one of the most dramatic scenes in *Uncle Tom's Cabin.* Few readers of the novel missed its point. If anyone tried to help Eliza and her baby, they would be guilty of violating the Fugitive Slave Act of 1850.[4]

Legend has it that after the start of the Civil War, Abraham Lincoln met with Harriet Beecher Stowe and he supposedly greeted her saying, "So you're the little lady whose book started this great war."

the book. Many white Southerners proclaimed the book was wholly untrue, and both northern and southern writers published many proslavery and "Anti-Tom" novels up to the beginning of the Civil War in 1861.[5]

Emancipation and Justice

And by virtue of the power . . . I do order and declare that all persons held as slaves . . . henceforward shall be free; and that the Executive government of the United States, including the military and naval authorities thereof, will recognize and maintain the freedom of said persons.[6]
—Abraham Lincoln's *Emancipation Proclamation*, 1863

The American Civil War officially began on April 12, 1861, when the South fired on Fort Sumter in South Carolina. Abraham Lincoln had only been president of the United States for a little over five months. Lincoln had been against slavery for a very long time. In 1831, when he was a young man, Lincoln told an audience in New Orleans, "If I ever get a chance to hit that thing [slavery], I'll hit it hard."[7] As the war progressed, Lincoln began thinking about issuing an emancipation proclamation. During the second Battle of Bull Run, in July 1862, Lincoln read his initial draft of the proclamation to men in his cabinet—the men could see a lot of thought had gone into this document.[8]

According to Thomas T. Eckert, who was in charge of the telegraph office in the War Department, Lincoln was a frequent visitor. The president would come almost every day to get reports on how the war was going. Lincoln liked to get away from the bustle of the White House for short periods of time. One morning in June,

Lincoln asked for some paper and sat down in Eckert's chair. Eckert recalled that:

> He would look out of the window a while . . . and then put his pen to paper, but he did not write much at once. He would study between times and when he had made up his mind he would put down a line or two, and then sit quiet for a few minutes. After a time he would resume his writing. . . .

Though Abraham Lincoln had always been opposed to slavery, he originally went to war to save the Union, not free the slaves. However, as the war progressed, he saw the need to free all those who were enslaved.

That first day, Lincoln did not write enough to fill even a sheet of paper. Before Lincoln left, he asked Eckert to keep his writing and not show it to anyone, so the paper was locked in a desk. Eckert remembered that, "This he did every day for several weeks." Each day Lincoln read over what he had written the day before, "studying carefully each sentence." Eckert did not know what the president was writing, until one day Lincoln told him he had been writing an order "giving freedom to the slaves in the South for the purpose of hastening the end of the war."[9]

Lincoln knew that issuing this proclamation would inflame the South. Southern gentlemen had seemed eager for war and many had fantasies of a race war between whites and blacks. Southerners feared slave rebellions, even as they insisted their slaves were loyal to them and would never leave the plantation. But, as soon as the war began, slaves were avid students of war news. House servants strained to overhear conversations by their masters about the war and then would eagerly pass the information to the field hands. Every area had a few slaves who could read and could get hold of a newspaper. News of the war's progress spread from region to region along what the slaves called the "grapevine telegraph," meaning by word of mouth. Slaves developed a resourceful network for communicating information throughout the South and to the North and back again.[10] Lincoln finished his draft to free the slaves living in the rebellious southern states. The news was carried, not only from the telegraph office where the president spent so many weeks, but from the lips of one slave to another.

President Lincoln asked Frederick Douglass if he thought slaves would take the initiative once the proclamation was announced. He wondered, "How do we get the slaves to run away?" Douglass knew full well that slaves had been running away for hundreds of years. Now that the Confederacy was faltering, southern whites would finally find out the truth. Would their slaves stay and be faithful to their masters, or would they leave? Southerners found out very quickly. It did not matter if the slave owner was cruel or kind—the slaves left. However, in some cases they could not leave until the Union Army came through

This 1888 poster provides the text of the Emancipation Proclamation beneath a portrait of Abraham Lincoln.

and liberated them. Thousands joined the Union Army to fight against their former owners. One Carolina plantation owner cried, "We were all laboring under a delusion. I believed that these people were content, happy, and attached to their masters."[11] He had found out that he was wrong.

The Fighting Fifty-Fourth

With the appearance of black troops, it became clear that the Civil War had become a social revolution. Even though African Americans had fought in the American Revolution and the War of 1812, they had never been allowed to join the regular army. Now they were enlisting by the thousands. The sight of black troops inspired people still in slavery, and enraged whites, as the soldiers paraded down southern city streets.

The most famous black fighting unit was the Fifty-Fourth Regiment of Massachusetts Volunteers. They were the first and most decorated black combat infantry unit to fight for the Union, and they were under the command of Colonel Robert Gould Shaw. The black soldiers were recruited by Governor John A. Andrew of Massachusetts, who was a dedicated abolitionist. Recruiting posters for the Fifty-Fourth asked "Colored Men [to] Rally 'Round the Flag of Freedom!'" They offered "Pay, $13 a Month! Good Food & Clothing! State Aid to Families!" and an additional "Bounty [of] $100!"

Shaw was the wealthy twenty-five-year-old son of Boston abolitionist parents who were friends of Frederick

African-American soldiers played an important role in the Union's victory in the Civil War. Here, an unidentified African-American soldier poses in uniform.

Douglass. When he was in college, Shaw quit to join the Union forces and had fought at the bloody battle of Antietam. Later, after being assigned to the Fifty-Fourth and impressed with the ability of his black regiment, which included two of Douglass' sons, Shaw paraded his soldiers through Boston within one hundred days of assembling them. By July 16, 1863, the Fifty-Fourth had distinguished itself in battle by rescuing the Tenth Connecticut Regiment from a Confederate attack on James Island in South Carolina. Then, without food or sleep, the Fifty-Fourth marched forty-eight hours straight for an assault on Fort Wagner on July 18, the main fort guarding Charleston, the South's main port.

It was considered to be a suicide mission. After a bombardment that did little to weaken the forces in Fort Wagner, Colonel Shaw drew his sword and led his six hundred men in a direct charge into the bombs and bullets coming from the fort. Shaw died at the summit of the fort. Nearly half of his men were killed, wounded, or missing. The Confederates stripped Colonel Shaw's body and it was thrown into a grave with the bodies of his men. The Fifty-Fourth's courageous charge at Fort Wagner not only encouraged greater participation of black troops in the Union cause—Lincoln said the battle tipped the balance in favor of victory—but helped change the perception of blacks in America.[12]

An African-American Fight Song

The First Arkansas Colored Regiment marched into battle singing the "First Arkansas Marching Song," which was written by Captain Lindley Miller. Like the "Battle Hymn of the Republic," the song was written to the tune of "John Brown's Body." Below are the third and fourth stanzas of the song, along with the chorus.

We have done with hoeing cotton, we have done with hoeing corn,
We are colored Yankee soldiers, now, as sure as you are born;
When the masters hear us yelling, they'll think it's Gabriel's horn,
As it went sounding on.

CHORUS
Glory, glory, hallelujah
Glory, glory, hallelujah
Glory, glory, hallelujah
As we go marching on.

They will have to pay us wages, the wages of their sin,
They will have to bow their foreheads to their colored kith and kin,
They will have to give us house-room, or the roof shall tumble in!
As we go marching on.

CHORUS REPEATS[13]

After the War

The Thirteenth Amendment to the United States Constitution was passed on December 18, 1865 and states, "Neither slavery nor involuntary servitude, except as a punishment for crime whereof the party shall have been duly convicted, shall exist within the United States, or any place subject to their jurisdiction."[14]

The Civil War lasted four years and cost about 617,000 American lives. The war's end in 1865 was the end of over 250 years of slavery in North America. African Americans would begin a new kind of life in the United States, and create a new kind of history.[15] On June 13, 1866, the Fourteenth Amendment was

African Americans celebrate after the Thirteenth Amendment abolished slavery in the United States of America.

passed by Congress. It was deliberately written to "grant citizenship to and protect the civil liberties of recently freed slaves." The amendment barred any state from denying or hindering the privileges of any citizen of the United States. The states could not deprive any person of "his life, liberty, or property without due process of law" or keep from any person their rights to equal protection under the law.[16] The amendment was ratified by the states in 1868, making it a part of the Constitution.

Even with the passage of civil rights amendments after the Civil War, the deeper problems of racism and prejudice remained in America. White feelings of bigotry against African Americans continued to cause frustration and pain. Southern governments passed segregation laws called Jim Crow laws that forced African Americans to give up their seats on public transportation. Black children could not go to school with white children. African Americans were even forced to drink out of separate water fountains. The vote was also taken away from most African Americans in the Deep South by the passage of laws demanding black voters take complex tests that many whites could not pass or pay special taxes to vote. It was not until the 1964 Civil Rights Act was passed that racial discrimination in public places was against the law; that employers could not discriminate against African Americans looking for work; that the same rules applied for whites and blacks when the right to vote was involved—ninety-nine years after the end of the Civil War.

The Legacy of the Abolitionists

The fight against slavery has taught Americans that great wrongs can be set right with dedication and perseverance. It also teaches that people can work together across ethnic, racial, and gender lines to accomplish a just goal. The men and women who fought the battle against American slavery used all of their talents to make their dream become reality. True, it took a tragic and bloody war to disengage the South from its dependence on slavery, but then that confrontation had been predicted since the debates over the Declaration of Independence. The constant drumbeat of dissent by Americans living in the North and South kept the discussion alive, even through times when others tried to silence them.

> ## The fight against slavery has taught Americans that great wrongs can be set right with dedication and perseverance.

The abolitionists were brave people like Harriet Tubman, making her daring raids into the South to bring her family to safety in the North; Lucretia Mott defiantly going against conventional behavior to challenge society; William Lloyd Garrison tirelessly writing and lecturing to stir every last soul he met to action; William Still carefully taking down the oral histories of the runaways he helped; Elijah Lovejoy replacing one destroyed printing press with another until he himself was destroyed; and Frederick Douglass, who worked for true equality. These are the people who whisper to us from history, telling us to keep ever vigilant and fight for freedom and equality because, believe it or not, slavery is still with us.

In places like Sudan in Africa, military groups kidnap women and children and make them slaves. People are forced to work on Dominican sugar plantations, and child slavery exists in pockets of the Middle East. Even today, antislavery advocates are pushing tirelessly to end the practice of forced servitude in whatever form it takes. Just like Sojourner Truth, Harriet Beecher Stowe, John Brown, and all the others who gave their lives to end slavery in America, modern antislavery advocates seek justice around the world. It seems to be a never-ending fight, but individual rights for life, liberty, and the pursuit of happiness have always been worth it. For to value the freedom of every human being is the essence of everyone's chance at true happiness.

1565 Slavery begins in North America; the Spanish bring slaves to St. Augustine in what will later become Florida.

1619 First slaves in an English colony; twenty Africans arrive in Jamestown, Virginia.

1652 The colony of Rhode Island is the first to ban slavery.

1701 England becomes the main supplier of slaves in the New World.

1776 Signing of the Declaration of Independence.

1787 The Society for the Abolition of the Slave Trade is founded in England; Constitutional Convention is held in Philadelphia, Pennsylvania.

1791 Bill of Rights is adopted.

1797 Sojourner Truth is born.

1800 Gabriel's Conspiracy; John Brown is born.

1808 The United States outlaws the importation of slaves.

1811 Harriet Beecher Stowe is born.

1818 Frederick Douglass is born.

1820 Compromise of 1820.

1821 Harriet Tubman and William Still are born.

1822 Liberia founded as an African colony for free African Americans.

1831 The first issue of the abolitionist newspaper *The Liberator* is published.

1833 American Anti-Slavery Society formed.

1835–1836 Proposition to censor abolitionist literature by U.S. Postmaster General; Congress passes gag rule prohibiting the reading of antislavery petitions in Congress.

1836 Frances McIntosh is lynched.

1837 Editor Elijah Lovejoy is murdered.

1840 The trial of *Amistad* Africans begins; Liberty Party is established by the radical abolitionists; the term "Underground Railroad" is seen in print.

1849 Henry "Box" Brown escapes to Philadelphia concealed in a box; the twenty-six hour journey ends with historian and abolitionist William Still welcoming him to freedom.

1850 Compromise of 1850.

1852 *Uncle Tom's Cabin* is published.

1854 Republican Party is formed.

1857 "Bleeding Kansas."

1859 John Brown's raid at Harpers Ferry, Virginia.

1860 Abraham Lincoln is elected president.

1861 Civil War begins.

1863 Emancipation Proclamation goes into effect; the assault on Fort Wagner by the Fifty-Fourth Regiment ends in much loss of life.

1865 The end of the Civil War; Thirteenth Amendment to the Constitution—slavery is declared illegal.

Chapter One   The Death of Elijah Lovejoy

1. David Grimsted, *American Mobbing, 1828–1861: Toward Civil War* (New York: Oxford University Press, 1998), pp. 103–104.

2. Russel B. Nye, *A Baker's Dozen: Thirteen Unusual Americans* (East Lansing: Michigan State University Press, 1956), pp. 255–256.

3. Ibid., p. 257.

4. Ibid., p. 259.

5. Ibid., p. 261.

6. Russel B. Nye, *Fettered Freedom: Civil Liberties and the Slavery Controversy, 1830–1860* (East Lansing: Michigan State College Press, 1949), pp. 116–117.

7. Ibid., pp. 118–119

8. Irving H. Bartlett, *Wendell Phillips, Brahmin Radical* (Boston, Mass.: Beacon Press, 1961), pp. 48–49.

9. Wendell Phillips, *The Federal Observer,* n.d., "Growing Pains of the Republic (1833–1869)," <http://www.federalobserver.com/print.php?aid=1180> (August 9, 2005).

Chapter Two   Early American Abolitionists

1. "The Rise of Antislavery Thoughts: 1800–1860," *Digital History,* <http://www.digitalhistory.uh.edu/database/textbook_search.cfm?HHID=45> (August 10, 2005).

2. John Stauffer, "In the Shadow of a Dream: White Abolitionists and Race," *In Collective Degradation: Slavery and the Construction of Race* (The Fifth Annual Gilder Lehrman Center International Conference at Yale University, November 7–8, 2003), p. 3

3. Jack D. Marietta, "The Reader's Companion to American History," n.d., <http://college.hmco.com/history/readerscomp/rcah/html/ah_072800_quakers.htm> (August 16, 2005).

4. Ian Frederick Finseth, "'Liquid Fire Within Language Me': Language, Self and Society in Transcendentalism and Early Evangelicalism, 1820–1860," <http://xroads.virginia.edu/~MA95/finseth/evangel.html> (August 22, 2005).

5. Ibid.

6. Ibid.

7. Ibid.

8. Susan Jacoby, *Freethinkers: A History of American Secularism* (New York: Metropolitan Books, 2004), p. 68.

9. Jack Fruchman Jr., "Foreword," *In Common Sense, Rights of Man, and Other Essential Writings of Thomas Paine* (New York: Signet Classics, 2003), p. xv.

10. Jeanne Boydston, Oakes et al., *Making a Nation: The United States and Its People*, Vol. 1 (Upper Saddle River, N.J.: Pearson-Prentice Hall, 2004), p. 183.

11. Gary Williams, "George Mason and the Bill of Rights," *Advocates for Self-Government,* n.d., <http://www.self-gov.org/freeman/920503.htm> (August 25, 2005).

12. Boydston, et al., p. 173.

13. Williams.

14. Ibid.

15. The Library of Virginia, "Gabriel's Conspiracy: Death or Liberty," n.d., <http://www.lva.lib.va.us/whoweare/exhibits/DeathLiberty/gabriel> (August 27, 2005).

16. Boydston, et al., p. 201

17. "Rebel's Statement From Gabriel's Conspiracy," *Africans in America*, n.d., <http://www.pbs.org/wgbh/aia/part3/3h493t.html> (August 27, 2005).

Chapter Three   **American Attitudes Toward Slavery**

1. "The Tightening Vise of Slavery in British Colonial New York," *Slavery in New York*, n.d., <http://www.slaveryinnewyork.org/gallery_3.htm> (September 1, 2006).

2. Gordon S. Wood, *The Gilder Lehrman Institute of American History*, n.d., <http://www.gilder

lehrman.org/collection/docs_archive_wash2.htm>
(August 29, 2005).

3. William W. Freehling, "The Founding Fathers and Slavery," *In American Negro Slavery: A Modern Reader*, 3rd Ed. (New York: Oxford University Press, 1979), p. 9.

4. Eric Foner, *Free Soil, Free Labor, Free Men: The Ideology of the Republican Party Before the Civil War* (New York: Oxford University Press, 1970), pp. 11–13.

5. Edmund S. Morgan, *American Slavery, American Freedom* (New York: W. W. Norton & Company, 1975), p. 297.

6. "The Cotton Gin: Eli Whitney and the Need for an Invention," *The Eli Whitney Museum*, n.d., <http://www.eliwhitney.org/cotton.htm> (February 8, 2006).

7. Gavin Wright, *The Political Economy of the Cotton South: Households, Markets, and Wealth in the Nineteenth Century* (New York: W. W. Norton & Company, 1978), pp. 14–15.

8. Morgan, pp. 333–334.

9. John C. Calhoun, "Slavery, A Positive Good," *Douglass: Archives of American Public Address*, n.d., <http://douglassarchives.org/calh_a59.htm> (September 3, 2005).

10. "African American Mosaic: Colonization," *The Library of Congress*, n.d., <http://www.loc.gov/exhibits/african/afam002.html> (February 16, 2006).

11. "The Blessings of Slavery," *Douglass: Archives of American Public Address,* n.d., <http://douglassarchives.org/plai_a60.htm> (September 3, 2005).

12. Foner, pp. 15–21.

13. Clifford S. Griffin, *Their Brothers' Keepers: Moral Stewardship in the United States, 1800–1865* (New Brunswick, N.J.: Rutgers University Press, 1960), p. 43.

14. "The American Anti-Slavery Society," *USInfo. State.Gov,* n.d., <http://usinfo.state.gov/usa/infousa/facts/democrac/18.htm> (September 11, 2005).

15. Calvin Lane, "Lewis Tappan New York Merchant, and Abolitionist," *Exploring* Amistad *at Mystic Seaport,* ©1997, <http://amistad.mysticseaport.org/discovery/people/bio.tappan.lewis.html> (February 15, 2006.)

16. William Lloyd Garrison, "Selections from the Writings of W. L. Garrison," *Uncle Tom's Cabin and American Culture,* n.d., <http://jefferson.village.virginia.edu/utc/abolitn/abeswlgct.html> (September 11, 2005.)

Chapter Four   The Abolitionists

1. Frederick Douglass, "Various Incidents," *In Frederick Douglass: The Narrative and Selected Writings,* p. 353.

2. Ibid., p. 358.

3. William S. Connery, "Proud Lion of Baltimore: The Life and Legacy of Frederick Douglass," *World and I*, Vol. 18, February 2003, p. 156.

4. Frederick Douglass, *Frederick Douglass: The Narrative and Selected Readings* (New York: Random House, 1984), pp. 42–44.

5. Frederick Douglass, "Narrative of the Life of Frederick Douglass, An American Slave," May 17, 1997, *Berkeley Digital Library Sunsite*, <http://sunsite.berkeley.edu/Literature/Douglass/Autobiography/06.html> (February 12, 2006).

6. John Stauffer, "In the Shadow of a Dream: White Abolitionists and Race," *Collective Degradation: Slavery and the Construction of Race,* (The Fifth Annual Gilder Lehrman Center International Conference at Yale University, November 7–8, 2003), p. 11.

7. Connery, p. 156.

8. "Frederick Douglass: The Hypocrisy of American Slavery," *The History Place: Great Speeches Collection,* n.d., <http://www.historyplace.com/speeches/douglass.htm> (September 12, 2005.)

9. "Frederick Douglass", Africans in America, n.d., <http://www.pbs.org/wgbh/aia/part4/4p1539.html> (September 11, 2004).

10. Roseann M. Mandziuk and Suzanne Pullon Fitch, *Sojourner Truth as Orator: Wit, Story, and Song* (Westport, Conn.: Greenwood Press, 1997), p. 5.

11. Anne Wortham, "Sojourner Truth: Itinerant Truth-Teller," *World and I,* Vol. 15, March 2000, p. 291.

12. Jacqueline Bernard, *Journey Toward Freedom: The Story of Sojourner Truth* (New York: Feminist Press at the City University of New York, 1990), p. 126.

13. "Sojourner Truth", *Women in History,* n.d., <http://www.lkwdpl.org/wihohio/trut-soj.htm> (September 17, 2005).

14. Anne Wortham, "Sojourner Truth: Itinerant Truth-Teller," *World and I,* Vol. 15, March 2000, p. 291.

15. "Sojourner Truth," *Spartacus Educational,* n.d., <http://www.spartacus.schoolnet.co.uk/USAStruth.htm> (September 17, 2005).

16. Susan Jacoby, *Freethinkers: A History of American Secularism* (New York: Metropolitan Books, 2004), pp. 94–95.

17. "Provisions of the Compromise of 1850," *U-S-History.com,* n.d., <http//www.u-s-history.com/pages/h182.html> (February 13, 2006).

18. "Bleeding Kansas," *Africans in America,* n.d., <http://www.pbs.org/wgbh/aia/part4/4p2952.html> (February 13, 2006).

19. Henry D. Thoreau, "The Last Days of John Brown," *The Walden Woods Project,* <http://www.walden.org/Institute/thoreau/writings/essays/Last_Days.htm> (September 23, 2005).

20. Douglass, *Frederick Douglass: The Narrative and Selected Readings,* p. 183.

21. Stauffer, p. 19.

22. Douglass, *Frederick Douglass: The Narrative and Selected Readings*, pp. 184–187.

23. "The Raid on Harpers Ferry," *Africans in America*, n.d., <http://www.pbs.org/wgbh/aia/part4/4p2940.html> (October 1, 2005).

24. Daniel F. Rulli, "Robert E. Lee's Demand for the Surrender of John Brown," *Social Education*, Vol. 68, 2004, pp. 306–310.

25. "The Raid on Harpers Ferry."

26. Stephen D. Brown, "Ghosts of Harpers Ferry," n.d., <http://wesclark.com/jw/newby.html> (October 1, 2005).

27. "John Brown's Black Raiders," *Africans in America*, <http://www.pbs.org/wgbh/aia/part4/4p2941.html> (October 1, 2005).

28. Brown.

29. Lloyd Chiasson, Jr., ed., *The Press on Trial: Crimes and Trials as Media Events* (Westport, Conn.: Greenwood Press, 1997), p. 28.

30. John Brown, "American Memory," *Library of Congress*, n.d., <http://memory.loc.gov/ammem/today/oct16.html> (October 1, 2005).

31. Rulli, pp. 306–310.

Chapter Five   Antislavery Views in Print

1. "Postmaster General Amos Kendall's Report on the Delivery of Abolition Materials in the Southern States," *History Department* <http://history.furman.edu/~benson/docs/postal35.htm> (October 2, 2005).

2. Wendy McElroy, "The Post Office as a Violation of Constitutional Rights," *The Freeman-Ideas on Liberty, Foundation for Economic Education,* May 2001, <http://www.fee.org/vnews.php?nid=4935#2> (October 2, 2005).

3. "Struggles Over Slavery: The Gag Rule," *National Archives,* n.d., <http://www.archives.gov/exhibits/treasures_of_congress/text/page10_text.html> (October 2, 2005).

4. "John Quincy Adams: Gag Rule Tactics," *American Rhetorical Movements to 1900,* n.d., <http://www.wfu.edu/~zulick/340/gagrule2.html> (October 2, 2005).

5. Frederic Hudson, *Journalism in the United States, From 1690 to 1872* (London: Routledge/Thoemmes Press, 2004.), p. xvi.

6. Asa Earl Martin, "Pioneer Anti-Slavery Press," March 25, 2003, *Dinsmore Documentation,* <http://www.dinsdoc.com/martin-1.htm> (October 2, 2005).

7. Harriet Hyman Alonso, *Growing Up Abolitionist: The Story of the Garrison Children* (Amherst, Mass.: University of Massachusetts Press, 2002), p. 28.

8. Susan Jacoby, *Freethinkers: A History of American Secularism* (New York: Metropolitan Books, 2004), p. 83.

9. John Corrigan, *Business of the Heart: Religion and Emotion in the Nineteenth Century* (Berkeley, Calif.: University of California Press, 2002), p. 119.

10. Eric Foner, *Free Soil, Free Labor, Free Men: The Ideology of the Republican Party Before the Civil War* (New York: Oxford University Press, 1970), pp. 109–112.

11. "Little Laura, the Kentucky Abolitionist," *Antislavery Literature*, n.d., <http://antislavery.eserver.org/childrens/littlelaura> (October 3, 2005).

12. Deborah Gray White, "Let My People Go: 1804–1860," in *To Make Our World Anew: A History of African Americans,* eds. Robin D. G. Kelley and Earl Lewis (New York: Oxford University Press, 2000), p. 210.

13. A.G. Duncan, "Antislavery Hymn," *Old Sturbridge Village Research Library*, n.d., <http://www.osv.org/learning/Document Viewer.php?DocID=2087> (October 3, 2005).

14. "African American Odyssey," *American Memory, Library of Congress*, n.d., <http://memory.loc.gov/ammem/aaohtml/exhibit/aopart2b.html#0210> (October 2, 2005).

15. Waldo E. Martin, Jr., *The Mind of Frederick Douglass* (Chapel Hill: University of North Carolina Press, 1984), p. 18.

16. Ibid., p. 36.

Chapter Six   The Underground Railroad

1. Underground Railroad, *The Columbia Encyclopedia*, 6th ed. (New York: Columbia University Press, 2004), <http://www.bartleby.com/65/> (August 22, 2006).

2. John Hope Franklin and Loren Schweninger, *Runaway Slaves: Rebels on the Plantation* (Oxford, England: Oxford University Press, 1999), p. 116.

3. "Forever Free: Abraham Lincoln's Journey to Emancipation: Robert J. Levi Coffin. (1789–1877)," *Cincinnati Public Library*, n.d., <http://www.cincinnatilibrary.org/foreverfree/levicoffin.html> (October 3, 2005).

4. "Reminiscences of Levi Coffin; The Reputed President of the Underground Railroad; Being a Brief History of the Labors of a Lifetime in Behalf of the Slave, with the Stories of Numerous Fugitives, Who Gained Their Freedom Through His Instrumentality, and Many Other Incidents: Electronic Edition," *Documenting the American South*, 2001, <http://docsouth.unc.edu/nc/coffin/coffin.html> (October 3, 2005).

5. Ruth Bogin and Bert James Loewenberg, eds., *Black Women in Nineteenth-Century American Life: Their Words, Their Thoughts, Their Feelings* (University Park: Pennsylvania State University Press, 1976), p. 220.

6. Deborah Gray White, "Let My People Go: 1804–1860," in *To Make Our World Anew: A History of African Americans,* eds. Robin D. G. Kelley and Earl Lewis (New York: Oxford University Press, 2000), p. 194.

7. Ibid.

8. "Africans in America: Harriet Tubman," *Public Broadcasting System*, n.d., <http://www.pbs.org/wgbh/aia/part4/4p1535.html> (October 4, 2005).

9. William Loren Katz, "Excerpts from William Still's 'Underground Railroad,'" 2001, <http://www.undergroundrr.com/life2a.html> (October 4, 2005).

10. Willie Lee Rose, *A Documentary History of Slavery in North America* (London: University of Oxford Press, 1999), pp. 271–274.

11. Linn Washington, Jr., "The Chronicle of an American First Family: The Stills Have Been With Us for 350 Years, and Their Combination of Suffering and Accomplishment Is Almost Unparalleled in Our History," *William Still Underground Railroad Foundation, Inc.*, n.d. <http://www.undergroundrr.com/foundation/genealogy.htm> (October 4, 2005).

Chapter Seven   A Long Fight

1. Jeanne Boydston, Oakes et al., *Making a Nation: The United States and Its People*, Vol. 1 (Upper Saddle River, N.J.: Pearson-Prentice Hall, 2004), p. 278.

2. Prudence Crandall, "Women in American History: Prudence Crandall," n.d., <http://search.eb.com/women/articles/Crandall_Prudence.html> (October 5, 2005).

3. Boydston, et al., p. 327.

4. *Harriet Beecher Stowe Center*, n.d., <http://www.harrietbeecherstowe.org> (October 9, 2005).

5. "Uncle Tom's Cabin, A Publication as a Turning Point," n.d., <http://nationalhistoryday.org/03_educators/2000/uncletom.htm> (October 9, 2005).

6. "Emancipation Proclamation," *National Archives*, n.d., <http://www.archives.gov/exhibits/featured_documents/emancipation_proclamation/transcript.html> (October 9, 2005).

7. John Hope Franklin, *The Emancipation Proclamation* (Garden City, N.Y.: Doubleday, 1963), p. 31.

8. "Lincoln Papers: Emancipation Proclamation Time Line," *Library of Congress,* n.d., <http://memory.loc.gov/ammem/alhtml/almtime.html> (October 9, 2005).

9. Franklin, pp. 35–36.

10. James M. McPherson, "Top Gun," *The Nation*, June 14, 2004, <http://www.thenation.com/doc/20040614/mcpherson> (October 9, 2005).

11. Boydston, et al., p. 357

12. Stephen May, "Memorial Rises in Honor of Black Soldiers' Valor," *The Washington Times*, September 20, 1997, p. 3.

13. Susan-Mary Grant, "Pride and Prejudice in the American Civil War," *History Today*, Vol. 48, September 1998, pp. 41–48.

14. Legal Information Institute, "U.S. Constitution," n.d., <http://www.law.cornell.edu/constitution/constitution.amendmentxiii.html> (October 10, 2005).

15. "The Civil War," *Africans in America*, n.d.,
    <http://www.pbs.org/wgbh/aia/part4/4narr5.
    html> (October 10, 2005).

16. "Anti-Slavery Society," *Spartacus Educational,*
    n.d., <http://www.spartacus.schoolnet.co.uk/
    USAantislavery.htm> (October 10, 2005).

abolitionist—Before 1865, someone who wanted to end slavery.

Emancipation Proclamation—Executive order by President Abraham Lincoln that freed the slaves in the Confederate States of America; the formal proclamation was made on January 1, 1863.

The Enlightenment—An eighteenth century philosophy that emphasized reasoning over superstition; it fostered a belief in the natural rights of human beings and promoted a scientific approach to political and social issues.

Evangelicalism—An enthusiastic desire to spread the religious teachings of the New Testament and convert others to believing that only through Jesus Christ can they go to heaven after death.

Free Soil Party—A political party created in 1847 to oppose the extension of slavery into newly gained territories from Mexico. Eventually, the new Republican Party absorbed the members of the Free Soil Party in 1854.

Manifest Destiny—A nineteenth-century belief that the United States had the duty and God-given right to expand its territory and influence westward and throughout North America, even if force was necessary.

martyr—A person who suffers and/or dies while pursuing a cause.

Quaker—A member of the religious Society of Friends; a group founded in England in the seventeenth century they were the first group to speak out against American slavery.

Second Great Awakening—A period during the eighteenth and early nineteenth century in American history when people became more religious; in New England, the awakening inspired social activism particularly against slavery.

Underground Railroad—A system developed by abolitionists to help slaves to escape to freedom in Canada and the northern free states of America.

Brackett, Virginia. *John Brown: Abolitionist.* Philadelphia: Chelsea House Publishers, 2001.

Butler, Mary G. *Sojourner Truth: From Slave to Activist for Freedom.* New York: PowerPlus Books, 2003.

De Angelis, Gina. *Lucretia Mott.* Philadelphia: Chelsea House Publishers, 2001.

DeFord, Deborah H. *Life Under Slavery.* New York: Facts on File, 2006.

Fauchald, Nick. *William Lloyd Garrison: Abolitionist and Journalist.* Minneapolis, Minn.: Compass Point Books, 2005.

Haugen, Brenda. *Frederick Douglass: Slave, Writer, Abolitionist.* Minneapolis, Minn.: Compass Point Books, 2005.

———. *Harriet Beecher Stowe: Author and Advocate.* Minneapolis, Minn.: Compass Point Books, 2005.

Jurmain, Suzanne Tripp. *The Forbidden Schoolhouse of Prudence Crandall.* Boston: Houghton Mifflin, 2005.

Kilngel, Cynthia. *Harriet Tubman: Abolitionist and Underground Railroad Conductor.* Chanhassen, Minn.: Child's World, 2004.

Landau, Elaine. *Fleeing to Freedom on the Underground Railroad: The Courageous Slaves, Agents, and Conductors.* Minneapolis: Twenty-First Century Books, 2006.

———. *Slave Narratives: The Journey to Freedom.* New York: Franklin Watts, 2001.

McKissack, Patricia C., and Frederick L. McKissack. *Days of Jubilee: The End of Slavery in the United States.* New York: Scholastic Press, 2003.

Rockwell, Anne. *Only Passing Through: The Story of Sojourner Truth*. New York: Alfred A. Knopf, 2000.

Swain, Gwenyth. *President of the Underground Railroad: A Story About Levi Coffin*. Minneapolis, Minn.: Carolrhoda Books, 2001.

Taylor, Yuval, ed. *Growing Up in Slavery: Stories of Young Slaves as Told by Themselves*. Lawrence Hill, 2005.

Waldstreicher, David. *The Struggle Against Slavery: A History in Documents*. New York: Oxford University Press, 2001.

Williams, Carla. *The Underground Railroad*. Chanhassen, Minn.: Child's World, 2002.

The African-American Mosaic: Abolition
<http://www.loc.gov/exhibits/african/afam005.html>

American Abolitionism
<http://americanabolitionist.liberalarts.iupui.edu/>

Frederick Douglass: Abolitionist/Editor
A biography of Douglass on the University of
Rochester Web site <http://www.history.rochester
.edu/class/douglass/home.html>

973.711 Cloud Tapper,
CLO   Suzanne.

          The abolition of
          slavery.

$31.93   35017000762487

DATE			